Table of Co

GW00724727

Dear parents, grandparents, and teachers,

Children ask many questions. Sometimes the inquiries are about God and spiritual matters. They want to know who God is and what he does. While some questions are easy to answer, others may require a search. To simplify the search and help you and the children you love understand the character and personality of our Creator, I've written this book of simple Bible-based devotions entitled *What Is God Like?* I'm hoping it will make your teaching task more fun and less burdensome.

Each one-page devotion begins with a verse to think about and concludes with follow-up in the form of questions, suggested activities, and a prayer. Many of the simple activities encourage quiet learning times. For active interaction you may wish to do the more involved suggested activities.

This book is intended for young children three to seven years old. You or your child may write his name on the blank provided within each devotion. In this way, the book becomes uniquely individual. To encourage further participation, you may have your child draw a happy face or place a sticker at the top of the page to celebrate completing each story and/or activity.

What *is* God like? God is good and he loves us! I hope you enjoy reading these stories with your child.

— *Joan C. Webb*

THE FIRST WEEK
Genesis 1:1-29

The Lord says, "I made the light and the darkness. I made the earth. And I made all the people living on it." *Isaiah 45:1, 7, 12*

Long ago darkness covered the water and water was everywhere. Then God said, "Turn on the light." With the new light came the first morning. The next day God said, "Divide up that water." Now there was sky above the water. The next day God said, "Dry up some of that water." And God called the dried up area "earth." Then God said, "Let the earth make plants and seeds."

On the next day God said, "Bright light, shine in the day. Small light, shine at night." The next day God put fish in the sea and birds in the sky. "This is good," said God. The next day God filled the earth with animals. "I like this, too," said God. Then God said, "Now we'll make people. They'll take care of my world."

God stopped and looked around. "This is really good," he said.

_____, God did all this working and creating in six days. On the seventh and last day of the first week God rested. He made the whole world in one week.

Questions
1. What did God make? (Sun, sky, fish, birds, animals, people — any related answer is fine.)
2. Who liked everything he made? (God)

Activities
1. Name activities you do each morning and each night.
2. Name the days of the week.

Prayer
Dear God, you made a beautiful world. Help me to enjoy and take care of what you made. Amen.

A PRETTY WORLD
Genesis 1:26-31; 2:7-14

The skies and the earth belong to you. You made the world and everything in it. *Psalm 89:11*

God loves beautiful things. Do you? Everything God made that first week was beautiful. In the morning the sun came up over the hill and sparkled like diamonds on the water.

Bright red apples and pointy yellow bananas grew on tall trees. A daddy lion played gently with his baby cubs. Four fuzzy baby ducks followed behind a mommy duck. The man God made watched and smiled. "It's all very beautiful," he said.

"I made it for you and me to enjoy," said God. "So have fun. Be kind to the animals. Eat the vegetables and fruits. And share all the beauty with your children."

_____ , God loves beautiful things. He is pleased when we stop working and hurrying and watching TV to enjoy every lovely thing he made.

Questions
1. Who loves beautiful things? (God, you, your child)
2. What pleases God? (When we stop to enjoy every lovely thing God made)

Activities
1. Name a few animals that you might see this week.
2. Discuss what your family might do to help take care of the beautiful world God made.

Prayer
Dear God, I know you love beautiful things. So do I. You made a pretty world. Help me enjoy it and take care of it. Amen.

ONE MORE BEAUTIFUL IDEA
Genesis 2:15-24

Then the Lord God said, "It is not good for the man to be alone.
I will make a helper who is right for him." *Genesis 2:18*

"Adam, I'm giving you a job to do," said God. "You're now in charge of the Garden of Eden. Make sure the animals are fed and cared for. And while you're working, think up a name for each animal." Adam enjoyed his new job. But he was lonely.

"I don't think it's a good idea for you to be alone all the time, Adam," said God. "I'm going to make another person to live with you and help you."

_____ , God had one more beautiful idea. This time God made a woman. She didn't look or sound like the man.

They worked, played, ate, and lived together. God had made them for one another.

Questions
1. What was Adam's job? (To feed, care for, and name the animals)
2. Who was lonely? (Adam)
3. Whose beautiful idea was it to make a man and woman? (God's)

Activities
1. Discuss the jobs of each member of your family.
2. Have your child think of jobs he might like to do when he is a grown-up.

Prayer
Dear God, you always have good ideas. Working is one of your good ideas. Help me to do my jobs well. Creating men and women and boys and girls is another one of your good ideas. Thank you for making me a _____ (boy or girl). Amen.

NO LONGER PERFECT
Genesis 3:1-19

So one sin of Adam brought the punishment of death to all people.
But in the same way, one good act that Christ did
makes all people right with God. *Romans 5:18*

_____ , everything was perfect in the garden God made. Adam and Eve never argued or complained. It never rained. The animals never ran away. Adam never had a cold.

Then it happened. Everything changed. Adam and his wife didn't plan to do it. But . . .

A snake came to the woman. "Eat this fruit and you'll be smart like God," he said.

"But God told us not to," said Eve.

"He didn't really mean it," said the snake. "Just give it a try."

It was a beautiful tree, the fruit looked good, and Eve did want to be smart like God, so she took a big bite.

"Here, Adam, you try it, too," she said. Then Adam took a big bite.

That's when everything changed. God had given the man and woman a choice, and they made the wrong one. Sadness and hurt came to Adam and his wife when they disobeyed God. When sadness and pain came to the garden, it came to the whole world. Nothing was perfect anymore.

Even though they had disobeyed, God loved the man and woman he made. God loves us all the time.

Questions
1. When was everything perfect? (In the garden)
2. Is everything perfect now? (No)

Activities
1. Name ways our world is not perfect anymore.
2. Name ways God shows he loves us.

Prayer
Dear God, I know you love me even though I'm not perfect. I'm glad. Thanks. Amen.

THE FIRST FAMILY
Genesis 4:1, 2

God blessed them and said, "Have many children and grow in number." *Genesis 1:28*

_____ , God made the first mommy and daddy. The man's name was Adam. His wife's name was Eve. The name Eve means "living" or "life." The Bible says that Eve was the mother of all living people.

One day, Eve said, "Adam, good news! We're going to have a baby." Then Adam and Eve waited. Finally the baby was born. "It's a boy!" Eve said. "God gave us a son! Let's name him Cain."

Adam and Eve cared for little Cain. They hugged him and rocked him to sleep. Cain went everywhere with his mom and dad. They loved him. Every day the little boy grew. He learned to walk. He learned to say "ma-ma" and "da-da."

Then Eve had another baby boy. Now the family had four people in it: Adam, Eve, Cain, and baby Abel. "God gave us two little children to love," said Eve.

Families are God's idea. He loves and cares about families.

Questions
1. What was the good news that Eve told Adam? ("We're going to have a baby!")
2. What did Adam and Eve name their first son? (Cain)
3. Who was Abel? (Cain's baby brother)

Activities
1. Name the people in your family.
2. Count the people in your family.

Prayer
Dear God, you made Adam and Eve and you gave them two baby boys. I know that loving families make you happy. Thank you for my family. Amen.

CAIN AND ABEL
Genesis 4:2-7

You must decide whom you will serve. *Joshua 24:15*

Brothers Cain and Abel played games together and helped Daddy Adam and Mommy Eve. When Cain grew up, he became a farmer and took care of the gardens. When Abel grew up, he became a shepherd. He took care of the sheep.

Abel cared about God. He wanted to do what God said. Cain had a different idea. He thought that what he wanted to do was more important than what God wanted.

God was pleased when Abel chose to love him. God was not pleased when Cain decided not to love him. Then Cain was angry because God was not pleased.

God cared about Cain. "If you keep being angry," said God, "soon you will *like* doing wrong all the time. I have a way for us to be happy together. But you must decide what you want to do."

_____ , Cain acted as if he didn't hear God. God talked to Cain, but Cain didn't answer.

Questions
1. Who loved and obeyed God? (Abel)
2. Who did not answer God? (Cain)

Activities
1. Name some chores that shepherds and farmers do.
2. Draw a picture of Abel watching his sheep and Cain planting his vegetables.

Prayer
Dear God, you loved Abel and Cain. You wanted both of them to love you. Cain decided not to talk to you. But I have decided to love you and talk to you in prayer. Amen.

LET'S CALL UP GOD
Genesis 4:25, 26

They will call to me, and I will answer them. *Psalm 91:15*

"God has given us another baby boy," said Eve. "I'm so happy." Adam and Eve named the tiny baby boy Seth. They taught Seth about God. When Seth grew up and got married, he had a baby boy, too.

Seth and his family decided to call on God's name. They cared about God. They believed what God told them. They prayed and talked to God. Seth and his family called up God like we call up a friend on the telephone.

_____ , we can call up God, too. We "call him up" every time we pray to him.

God answers. He answers not by talking aloud to us, but in other ways. He answers through his words in the Bible. He answers by giving us love in our hearts for other people.

Sometimes it may seem like God is not answering, but he may just be saying, "Wait a little while." When God sent his son, Jesus, he talked to us in a very special way.

Questions
1. What did Adam and Eve name the new baby boy? (Seth)
2. What did Seth do when he grew up? (Married, had a baby boy)
3. Who started to call on God's name? (Seth's family)

Activities
1. Pretend to call a friend or relative on the phone to talk.
2. Draw a picture of a telephone. Color it your favorite color.

Prayer
I call on your name, Lord God. You promised in the Bible that you hear and answer me. I'm glad you hear me and care about me. Thank you. Amen.

13

GOD'S PLAN
Genesis 5:5, 27; 6:9-22

*"I have good plans for you. I don't plan to hurt you.
I plan to give you hope." Jeremiah 29:11*

_____ , how old are you? How old is Grandpa? The first man, Adam, lived to be 930 years old. That's really old!

Adam had lots of grandchildren and great grandchildren. They all lived long lives. His great-great-great-great-great grandson Methuselah was the oldest man who ever lived.

The people lived long lives, but there was a BIG problem. The people forgot God. God had given them air to breathe, food to eat, and a beautiful world to enjoy, yet they cheated, lied, and hurt one another. God was sad. "I'm sorry I ever made men and women," said God. "I'll take them off my earth."

One man loved God. His name was Noah. "I have a plan for you, Noah," said God. "I want you to build a boat. Bring a boy and girl animal of every kind with you on the boat. It's going to rain. Water will cover the earth. When the rains come, your family and the animals will be safe inside the boat." So Noah and his family started hammering.

God had a plan for Noah. God has a plan for us, too. Part of his plan is for us to learn to love and believe him.

Questions
1. Who was the oldest man who ever lived? (Methuselah)
2. What was the big problem? (The people forgot God.)
3. Who loved God? (Noah)
4. What was God's plan for Noah? (To build the big boat)

Activity
Pretend to build a big boat.

Prayer
Dear God, I know you have a good plan for me. I love you and believe you. Amen.

WHO SHUT THE DOOR?
Genesis 7:1-16

It was by faith that Noah . . . obeyed God and built a large boat
to save his family. *Hebrews 11:7*

Noah built a BIG boat just like God told him to do. Boy and
girl animals of every kind came to get on the boat. Noah made
sure there was food for everyone. Then he waited.

_____ , how do you feel when you have to wait? (Pause
for response.) It's hard to wait sometimes, isn't it?

"Noah, it's time! "
God said finally.
"Take your family
and the animals
and get into the
boat. Then wait
seven more days
and I'll send rain."

Noah obeyed
God. Mice and rab-
bits, elephants and giraffes, lions and monkeys, kittens and pup-
pies all marched into the ark. When everyone was in the boat, God
shut the door.

God kept Noah, his family, and the animals safe inside the
boat. Noah waited and believed God even when it was hard. We
can learn to wait and believe in God, too. He will take care of us.

Questions
1. Who obeyed God? (Noah)
2. Who shut the door of the ark? (God)

Activities
1. Name some animals that Noah took on the boat with him.
2. Pretend the bed is the ark. Climb onto the bed and sit together
   with all your stuffed animals. Pretend to wait for the rain.
   Watch for lightning; listen for thunder. Pray the following
   prayer while you're on the "boat."

Prayer
Dear God, Noah believed and obeyed you. We trust you, too.
Please keep us safe. Amen.

THE LONG BOAT RIDE
Genesis 7:11, 12; 8:1-20

Then Noah built an altar to the Lord. *Genesis 8:20*

Seven days after Noah's family climbed into the big boat, it rained. And then it rained some more. For 40 days and nights it rained. It rained so hard and long that the ground began to look like a huge swimming pool. Water covered the housetops, tree-tops, and mountaintops.

One day Noah felt a jolt. What do you think happened? (Pause for a response. Any response is fine.) The big boat hit a mountain peak and stopped. Every day after that the waters went down. Finally, Noah opened a window. The fresh air felt good. Noah sent a bird out the window, but it flew back. It couldn't find dry land. Noah sent another bird. It came back, too. Then Noah sent another bird. It came back carrying a leaf in its beak. A few days later Noah sent out another bird. This time, the bird found a place to build a nest and never came back.

"OK, Noah," said God. "It's safe to leave now." For one year and one week Noah and his family had lived inside the boat. _____ , how do you think they felt when they walked outside for the first time in a whole year? What do you think they did?

Questions
1. How long did it rain? (40 days and nights)
2. Who sent a bird out the boat's window? (Noah)
3. How long did Noah's family and the animals stay on the boat? (One year and one week)

Activities
1. Make sounds like the birds singing.
2. Pretend to sway with the waves.

Prayer
Dear God, thank you for saving Noah's family and the animals. And thank you for watching over me, too. Amen.

RAINBOW ON THE RIVER
Genesis 9:12-17

I am putting my rainbow in the clouds. It is the sign
of the agreement between me and the earth.
Genesis 9:13

Richie and his family drifted down the river in their boat. It had rained earlier and now a soft breeze blew across their faces. "Look," said Richie. "It's a rainbow!" Mom, Dad, and little sister Lynnette turned to see a rainbow stretched across the sky from the treetops on one side of the river to the hilltops on the other.

"There are two rainbows!" shouted Lynnette. "Aren't they pretty?"

"Tell us about the first rainbow," said Richie.

"Noah, his family, and all the animals took a long boat ride during the flood," said Mom. "Finally God told them they could all leave the boat and get on dry land," said Mom. "They were happy to be alive and safe."

"Then they stopped to thank God for keeping them safe," said Dad. "And God said, 'Never again will I flood the whole earth. I'm sending you rainbows in the sky so you'll remember my promise.'"

_____ , the next time you see a colorful rainbow in the sky, remember that God loves you and will always keep his promises.

Questions
1. Who drifted down the river in a boat? (Richie and his family)
2. Why does God make rainbows? (To remind us that he loves us and that he'll never flood the whole earth again!)

Activities
1. Name the colors found in a rainbow.
2. Draw or color a rainbow.

Prayer
Dear God, thank you for the pretty colors in the rainbow. Thank you for all your promises. Amen.

BUILDING A TOWER TO HEAVEN
Genesis 11:1-9

The nations must learn that they are only human. *Psalm 9:20*

_____ , it's hard to talk to someone if you can't understand what he's saying, isn't it? Many years ago all the people on earth sounded alike. They all spoke the same language. One day they said, "Let's build a huge city to show how important we are. We'll make a tall tower that reaches to Heaven. We'll all live together in the big city."

God had told the people to spread out and start new cities on the earth. But the people didn't obey God. They thought they had a better idea than God.

"The people think they don't need me," said God. "I'm going to change their language so they can't understand one another."

God changed the people's one language into many languages. The people moved away from each other and went to live in other cities. They stopped building the tall tower. They learned that men and women, boys and girls should not try to be bigger and stronger than God. God made us, and we are happier when we live by God's ideas.

Questions
1. What did the people try to do? (Build a big city and tower to Heaven so they could all live in the same place)
2. Who changed the people's words and languages? (God)

Activities
1. Name a few languages or countries of today. (Ideas: Spain, Germany, Japan)
2. Say a word from another language. (Examples: *Adios* is the Spanish word for "good-bye" and *liebe* is German for "love.")

Prayer
Dear God, I want to obey you. I want to be happy living by your ideas. Amen.

TALKING WITH GOD
Genesis 12:6-8

I prayed to you with all my heart. *Psalm 119:58*

_____ , traveling can make a person tired, can't it? Abraham and Sarah traveled a long time. They were probably very tired when they stopped under a big tree in a place called Shechem. God came to Abraham there and said, "Look around you, Abraham. I'm going to give this land to your children and grandchildren."

Abraham didn't understand what God was saying. Other people lived in this place. Abraham and Sarah had no children. There seemed to be lots of reasons why it would not work for God to give the land to Abraham and his children. But Abraham listened to God. He built an altar to mark the place where God talked with him.

Abraham and Sarah moved on. When they stopped again, Abraham built another altar. There he prayed to God. He knew he needed to keep talking to God. He knew God was going to do something very special in his life.

Questions
1. Who built two altars? (Abraham)
2. What did Abraham do at the altars? (Talk to God and listen to God)

Activities
1. Walk your two fingers up your arm and talk about the long trip that Abraham and his family took.
2. Build a pretend altar out of blocks or boxes. (In Abraham's day, an altar was often made out of rocks piled on top of each other.)

Prayer
Dear God, just like Abraham, I will keep talking to you. I want to know more about what you want me to be and do. Please help me. Thank you. Amen.

LYING ISN'T A GOOD IDEA
Genesis 12:10-20

Do not lie to each other. *Colossians 3:9*

_____ , do you know what it means to tell a lie? To tell a lie is to say something that is not true. Abraham told a lie. Let me tell you the story. Abraham and his neighbors were hungry. There was no food in the land. So Abraham and Sarah went to Egypt to get food. Abraham said, "Sarah, you're so beautiful that the king will want you to live with him. He'll hurt me if he thinks I'm your husband. Tell him you're my sister. That will be better for me."

It happened the way Abraham said it would. The king of Egypt liked Sarah. But God didn't want Sarah to be with Pharaoh, and the king got sick. "Something is wrong here," he said. "Call Abraham."

"Why did you say that Sarah is your sister?" asked the king. "I know she's your wife. Take her back. Leave Egypt. You made trouble for us by telling a lie."

God wants us to tell the truth. Even when we think it would be better to lie, God wants us to be truthful. God always tells the truth. He wants us to tell the truth, too.

Questions
1. Why did Abraham and Sarah leave their land? (There wasn't any food.)
2. Who wants us to tell the truth? (God)

Activity
Talk about some times when you thought about telling a lie.

Prayer
Dear God, I know it's best to tell the truth. Help me to have courage to tell the truth. Amen.

COMING BACK TO GOD
Genesis 13:1-4

Come back to God, and he will forgive your sins. *Acts 3:19*

_____ , how do you feel after you've disobeyed Mom or Dad? Are you sad? Do you want to talk with them and make everything right again? Perhaps this is how Abraham felt after he lied to the king of Egypt.

The king said, "Abraham, go away." So Abraham took Sarah and all his servants and animals and moved back to Bethel. Bethel was the place where Abraham built an altar to God. It was the same place he prayed and talked to God before. Now he came to the altar again and called on the name of God.

We don't know the exact words Abraham prayed. Maybe he prayed something like this: "Dear God, I lied to the king of Egypt. I know it wasn't the right thing to do. I'm sorry. Please forgive me.

Help me not to do it again. I know you'll take care of me, even in the middle of hungry times like the famine. You're very good to me. Thanks. Amen."

No matter what we do, whether it's good or bad, God always loves us. God will always listen when we ask him to forgive us.

Questions
1. Who told Abraham to leave Egypt? (The king of Egypt)
2. Where did Abraham go after he left Egypt? (To the altar at Bethel)
3. Whom did Abraham talk to? (God)

Activities
1. Fold your hands in prayer to God.
2. Draw a picture of Abraham praying to God.

Prayer
Dear God, I know I can pray to you anytime. You love me always, even when I lie. I know you will forgive me when I ask. Amen.

JUICY GREEN GRASS
Genesis 13:1-13; 2 Peter 2:7, 8

When you do things, do not let selfishness or pride be your guide.
Philippians 2:3

"Get out of my way!" yelled Lot's shepherd. Lot was Abraham's nephew. "Your sheep are hoggin' all the grass."

"Well, my sheep have to eat, too, ya know," shouted Abraham's man.

"There's no room for your sheep and cows here," screamed Lot's shepherd. "So get lost."

"We'll just see about that," answered Abraham's man. "I'm going to talk to my boss."

Abraham learned about the fights between his men and Lot's men. "We both have lots of cows, sheep, and workers," Abraham said to Lot. "But we're running out of room. Our workers shouldn't be fighting. It might be best if we stopped living together. See all that land out there? You choose what part you want. Whatever you take, I'll take the other side."

Lot looked all around. The land by the Jordan Valley had juicy green grass. It was the best land. "I'll live there," said Lot as he pointed to the valley.

So Lot got the best land. But there was one problem. The people in the city next to the valley didn't care about God. After a while, Lot became sad about his selfish decision.

_____ , it is a good idea to ask God to help us make smart and unselfish choices.

Questions
1. Who fought with words? (Abraham's and Lot's men)
2. Who took the best land for himself? (Lot)

Activity
Pretend to mow the tall green grass.

Prayer
Dear God, please help me to make smart and unselfish decisions.

BELIEVING GOD'S PROMISES
Genesis 13:14-18

Abraham never stopped believing. *Romans 4:20*

_____ , have you ever felt sad when you moved away from a friend you loved? Or maybe your friend or neighbor moved away from you? When Lot and Abraham moved away from each other, maybe Abraham was sad. Maybe he missed his nephew, Lot.

After Lot moved, God said to Abraham, "Look around. Look to your right. Look to your left. All the land you see I'll give to you and your children. Your children will have children and they will have children and then *they* will have children until there are so many people no one will be able to count them all. Go now. Walk around on this land. I promise I'll give it to you."

So Abraham walked through the land. He walked over the hills and over the rocks. He walked past the trees and down the roads. Then he moved his tent house to a place called Hebron. There he prayed and remembered God's promise. He believed all that God told him.

Questions
1. Who promised to give Abraham all the land? (God)
2. Who believed God? (Abraham)

Activities
1. Hold up your right hand. Hold up your left hand.
2. Color two empty cardboard rolls. (Use empty paper towel or bathroom tissue rolls.) Tape the sides together. Attach a string or ribbon to one end of each roll. Now hang them around your neck. Hold them up to your eyes. Look through them. Pretend you can see as far as Abraham did.

Prayer
Dear God, Abraham believed your promise to him. He never stopped believing. Help me to believe you, too. Amen.

HELPING OTHERS
Genesis 14:1-14

Help each other with your troubles. *Galatians 6:2*

Lot lived in a beautiful place. His sheep walked along the river and ate juicy green grass. His wife and children had many friends. Lot worked in the city. They all were very busy. But there was fighting near their town of Sodom. Four kings from one side fought against five kings from another side. One day the armies came to Sodom. They took all the furniture and food from the houses. The soldiers took Lot and his family away. They were prisoners!

At the same time, Abraham lived in another city. Abraham was a good man. He treated people with kindness. Everyone knew Abraham loved and prayed to God. A man who knew both Lot and his uncle Abraham ran straight to Abraham. "Lot and his family have been taken away," he said.

When Abraham heard the news, he hurried to get Lot and his family away from the soldiers. Lot couldn't help himself this time. He needed Abraham's help.

At times our friends may need help. When one of our friends can't help himself, we can be his helper. God will help us help others.

Questions
1. Who lived in Sodom? (Lot and his family)
2. Who loved and prayed to God? (Abraham)

Activity
Plan to help someone who cannot help himself. (Ideas: Take food to a hungry person; read to a blind person; visit someone who is sick and cannot get out; baby-sit for a tired mother.)

Prayer
Dear God, Abraham was ready to help when Lot needed him. Please help me to be ready to help when someone needs me.

HE'S MY GOD, TOO!
Genesis 14:14-16

The Lord gives strength to his people. *Psalm 29:11*

Abraham called a meeting of the 318 men who worked for him. "Listen, men, my friend and nephew Lot is in BIG trouble. There is fighting where he lives. He and his family have been taken away from their home. I want to go get them. Will you go with me?"

"Yes, Abraham, we'll go," said the men. They liked Abraham. He was kind. They knew Abraham loved God. They knew Abraham's God was very strong and powerful. They believed God would help Abraham get Lot and his family out of the war.

"Let's surprise the people," Abraham said. "We'll go at night. They won't be looking for us then." Abraham's idea worked! God helped Abraham and his men.

_____ , Abraham's God is the same God who made the world. He is the same God who made you and me. He helps us today just as he helped Abraham many years ago.

Questions
1. How many men did Abraham take with him? (318)
2. Did Abraham go to get Lot during the day or the night? (Night)
3. Who helped Abraham and the men get Lot and his family? (God)

Activity
Turn the lights off for a few minutes (or close your eyes tightly). Think about how it would be to work or fight the army in the dark (at night).

Prayer
Dear God, you are the God of Abraham and you are my God, too. You are strong and have all power. Amen.

FORGIVING IS BEST
Genesis 13:10-12; Genesis 14:14, 15

If someone does wrong to you, do not pay him back
by doing wrong to him. *Romans 12:17*

"Ha, ha! You got in trouble. You didn't share," yelled Jeremy.
His friend, Peter, looked down at the floor. He needed Jeremy's
love and forgiveness, not mean words. To forgive means to stop
being mad at someone. It means that we say, "I know you did
wrong to me and it hurt, but I will keep loving you."

This short story shows what sometimes happens when friends
aren't nice to each other. But Abraham was different. He didn't act
like Jeremy. Abraham found out that his friend and nephew, Lot,
was in big trouble. So he went to help him.

Abraham could have said, "Well, Lot, you're the one who
decided you wanted the juicy grass for your animals. You were
selfish and didn't share with me. I guess I'll just let you stay in
trouble." But Abraham didn't say this. He knew Lot needed his
help. He believed God wanted him to help Lot and his family. So
Abraham showed love. He forgave Lot. God was pleased with
Abraham's decision. And God is pleased with us when we decide
to forgive and care about our friend even when he does wrong to
us.

Questions
1. Did Jeremy's mean words help Peter feel better? (No)
2. Did Abraham help Lot when he needed it? (Yes)

Activities
1. Make a sad face, a yelling face,
   and a loving and happy face.
2. Draw a picture of Jeremy
   yelling at Peter. Draw another
   picture of Jeremy forgiving
   Peter.

Prayer
Dear God, Abraham loved and
forgave Lot. I want to be a forgiving friend like Abraham. Please
help me. Amen.

WINNING AND REWARDS
Genesis 14:17, 21-24

God said, ". . . I will give you a great reward." *Genesis 15:1*

_____ , it feels good to win a game or contest, doesn't it? Abraham and his men were happy when they won and got Lot and his family back.

The king of Sodom was glad, too. He ran to thank Abraham for getting back all the people, food, furniture, and clothes the other kings had taken. "Give me back the people you rescued, and you can keep everything else," said the king.

But Abraham said, "I've talked to the Lord my God about this. I told him I wouldn't take anything from Sodom. I won't even take a shoe. I never want anyone in Sodom to say I got rich because I kept what was yours." Abraham had not helped Lot just so he could get rich or famous. He only wanted to do what God wanted. That is the reason Abraham didn't keep any of the food, clothing, or furniture for himself.

After the king left, God said, "Abraham, don't worry. I'll take care of you. I'll give you everything you need. And I will reward you. "

Questions
1. What king was happy when Abraham won the fight? (The king of Sodom)
2. Did Abraham keep the food, furniture, and clothes? (No)

Activities
Dress up like a king (with robe, crown, jewels, etc.).

Prayer
Dear God, Abraham didn't think that he should have gifts just because he did a good thing. I want to help others, too, without expecting that I'll get something special in return. Help me. Amen.

WHO IS MELCHIZEDEK?
Genesis 14:18-20

Our help comes from the Lord, who made heaven and earth.
Psalm 124:8

_____ , do you remember when the king of Sodom ran to thank Abraham? Another king came to meet Abraham, also. His name was Melchizedek (pronounced mel-KIZ-uh-dek). He was the king of Salem, but he was also a priest. He came to Abraham, bringing bread and drink. Melchizedek loved God just like Abraham did.

"Abraham, may God give you blessings," said Melchizedek. "The same God who made heaven and earth is our God. We praise him. We worship him. He helped you get Lot back. He helped you win the fight."

Abraham knew Melchizedek cared about God and listened to God. Melchizedek's special words pleased Abraham. Abraham decided to give Melchizedek a tenth of everything he had. Abraham believed Melchizedek loved God as he did.

Questions
1. What two kings came to Abraham? (The king of Sodom and the king Melchizedek of Salem)
2. Say "Melchizedek." (mel-KIZ-uh-dek)
3. What did Abraham give Melchizedek? (A tenth of all that he had)

Activities
1. Count 10 pennies. Put one penny aside. This is how much Abraham gave to Melchizedek out of every 10 pennies he had.
2. Draw a picture of 10 bananas or oranges. Cover one with your hand. The nine that you see is how much Abraham had left for himself after he gave one to Melchizedek.

Prayer
Dear God, Melchizedek and Abraham praised you. They loved you. I love you and praise you, too. Amen.

SINGING AND PRAISING
Exodus 15:1, 21; Psalm 149:1-5

Sing a new song to the Lord. Sing his praise in the meeting of his people. *Psalm 149:1*

_____ , do you know what a choir is? A choir is many people singing a special song together. There are grown-up choirs, teenage choirs, women's choirs, and men's choirs. There are also children's choirs. Have you ever sung in a children's choir?

Susie and Sandy are twin sisters. They look alike. They sing in the children's choir at the downtown church. "Today is choir day, Mom," said Susie. "When can we go?"

"After dinner the church bus will come get you. We'll walk to the corner and I'll wait with you," said Mom.

Sandy and Susie jumped up and down. They liked to sing. They liked to go to choir practice. Next Sunday was a special day. The children's choir planned to sing in the Sunday morning worship meeting. All the moms and dads, grandpas and grandmas, and big brothers and sisters would see and hear the children sing a new song to God.

God likes our singing. Isn't it fun to sing songs to God?

Questions
1. What were the names of the twin sisters? (Susie and Sandy)
2. What is a choir? (A choir is many people singing.)
3. Does God like our singing? (Yes)

Activities
1. Listen to a record, tape, or CD of a choir singing.
2. Try to sing the song you heard on the record, tape, or CD.

Prayer
Dear God, I will sing a song to you at home and at church. Singing makes me feel happy. I know that you like singing, too. Thank you for making songs and music. Amen.

IT'S HARD TO WAIT!
Genesis 16:1-3, 15, 16; Genesis 17:18, 19

Wait for the Lord's help. *Psalm 27:14*

_____ , do you get tired of waiting for your birthday to come? Do you sometimes get tired of wait ing for grandma to visit? It's hard to wait when you want something very much.

Abraham and Sarah were tired of waiting. They wanted a baby. They believed God told the truth when he promised them a baby boy. But they had waited ten years. Where was the baby?

One day, Sarah said, "Maybe we should adopt a baby. If my maid, Hagar, has a baby boy, let's call him our boy. Let's raise him to be the son God was telling us about."

So Hagar had a baby boy named Ishmael. Abraham loved this boy. But God said, "Abraham, Ishmael is not the special baby I promised to you. You and Sarah will have a baby boy next year."

Sometimes it is hard to wait. It was hard for Abraham and Sarah to wait. It is hard for you and me to wait. Many times we want God to hurry up and do what he promises. But God knows best. He can help us when we need to wait.

Questions
1. Who was tired of waiting for a baby? (Abraham and Sarah)
2. Who promised Abraham and Sarah a baby? (God)
3. Who said, "Let's adopt Hagar's baby boy"? (Sarah)

Activities
1. Name times we may have to wait. (Ideas: for dinner, for vacation, for Christmas, for baby sister or brother to be born, for Dad or Mom to come home, to get well when we have a cold)
2. Name times we might wait for God. (Ideas: For our friend to love Jesus, for God to answer a prayer)

Prayer
Dear God, help me to learn to wait quietly. Amen.

PRAYING FOR OTHERS

Genesis 18:17-33; Genesis 19:29

Pray for each other. *James 5:16*

_____ , have you ever prayed to God for someone else? Abraham did.

One day God said, "Abraham, the people who live in the city of Sodom don't care about me. They do really bad things. A sad thing is going to happen to that city."

"Lord, my friend and nephew, Lot, lives in Sodom. I don't want him to get hurt when something happens to the city. Please save him and anyone else who cares about you," prayed Abraham.

"OK, Abraham, I'll save all the people in Sodom who care about me," answered God.

God helped Lot, and he was saved from being hurt. Abraham cared enough to pray for his friend, Lot. You and I can pray for other people, too. God is happy when we pray to him. He wants us to pray for our friends.

Questions
1. Who said that the people of Sodom did really bad things? (God)
2. Who prayed for his friend and nephew Lot? (Abraham)

Activities
1. Name two friends that you can pray for.
2. Name people in your family you can pray for. (Fill in the blanks below with your friends' or family's names.)

Prayer
Dear God, please help _____ , _____ , _____ , and _____ in everything they do tomorrow. Thank you. Amen.

Note to parents/teachers
Abraham asked God to keep the city of Sodom safe if there were 50 good and God-loving people there. But there were not even 10 Sodomites who loved God.

GOD IS PATIENT
Genesis 20:1-17

But if we confess our sins, he will forgive our sins. *1 John 1:9*

_____ , do you remember the story about Abraham telling a lie? He told the king that Sarah was his sister. The king found out about the lie and made Abraham and Sarah get out of Egypt. God knew about Abraham's lie, too.

It seems that Abraham should have learned never to lie again. But when he moved to a new city, he said, "Sarah is not my wife. She's my sister." Abraham was afraid he'd get hurt if he told the truth. Maybe he forgot God promised to always take care of him.

This time the king didn't say, "Get out of here!" like before. The king said, "Take your wife back. You can stay here on my land and live anywhere you want to."

Then Abraham prayed. Perhaps Abraham said, "Lord, I'm sorry. I lied again. Please forgive me. And please help the king and his family, too."

God is sad when we decide to lie. But he is patient with us even when we forget and do it again. We can always come and talk to him again.

Questions
1. What did Abraham do just like before? (He lied about Sarah.)
2. Where did the king say Abraham could live? (Anywhere on his land)
3. Did Abraham pray to God? (Yes)

Activity
Draw a picture of Abraham talking to God.

Prayer
Dear God, I know you're sad when I forget to tell the truth. But I also know you love me and you forgive me when I say I'm sorry. I want to thank you for that. Amen.

GOD LIKES BABIES
Genesis 21:1-7

Children are a gift from the Lord. Babies are a reward.
Psalm 127:3

_____ , do you like babies? God likes babies, too.

Babies are fun to cuddle, play with, and love. Sometimes babies sleep; at other times they cry. Sometimes babies giggle; other times they fuss.

Babies need big people to take care of them. When babies come into the world, they don't know how to eat or talk or walk or work or play. Big brothers and sisters, grandmas and grandpas, aunts and uncles, and most of all, moms and dads, help little babies learn.

Sarah and Abraham had a baby boy named Isaac. Sarah and Abraham hugged Isaac. They wrapped him in warm blankets and rocked him to sleep. They kept him safe. They never left Isaac alone in their house-tent.

Sarah and Abraham sang and prayed with Isaac. They wanted their son to know about God. Years before Isaac was born, God had told Abraham and Sarah they would one day have a baby boy. They waited and waited. When Isaac came, they laughed for joy. Do you think they told young Isaac about God's promise all those years before? I think they did.

We can share the promises God makes to us, too. His promises are written in the Bible. It's never too early to tell our baby brothers and sisters about God.

Questions
1. Who likes babies? (God, grandma, grandpa, you and I)
2. What did Sarah and Abraham name their baby boy? (Isaac)

Activities
1. Hug your child.
2. Name some babies that your child might know.
3. Tell your child about the day he was born.

Prayer
Dear God, I know you like babies. I was a baby once. Now I'm growing up. Thanks for liking and loving me still. Amen.

THE STORY OF JOSEPH
Genesis 37:1-36; 39:1-21; 41:43; 45:1-9; 50:15-24

It is God who makes us able to do all that we do. *2 Corinthians 3:5*

"Don't leave me here alone," said Joseph. But his big brothers acted like they didn't hear. They threw Joseph in a deep hole. Joseph's ten older brothers didn't like him. So they sold Joseph to some strangers. Then they lied and told their father that a wild animal killed Joseph.

The strangers took Joseph to another land. After a while, Joseph got a job working for an important man named Potiphar. Joseph was strong and handsome. Everyone liked him. And God helped Joseph do a good job at everything. Then one day a woman tricked Joseph. She blamed Joseph for something he didn't do, and he was thrown into jail. But God helped Joseph there, too. When Joseph finally got out of prison, he went to work for the king.

One day Joseph's brothers came to buy food from Joseph. Joseph knew his brothers right away. But they didn't know him. "I'm your brother Joseph," he said. The brothers shook with fear. "Don't worry. I'm not mad," he said. "You wanted to hurt me, but God turned your mean actions into something good. I'm helping many people here. That was God's plan."

_____ , in the good and the bad times, God was with Joseph. It is God who helps us do what we need to do.

Questions
1. Who sold Joseph? (His ten older brothers)
2. Who was with Joseph during all the good and bad times? (God)

Activities
1. Hug your child like Joseph's dad hugged him.
2. Count to ten. (Joseph had ten older brothers.)

Prayer
Dear God, thank you for helping us to do what we need to do each day. Amen.

COMING HOME!
Genesis 46:29

*Let the Lord watch over us while we are separated
from each other. Genesis 31:49*

_____ , has someone you know ever moved away? You missed that person, didn't you? Larry's Uncle George moved away. He went to work in a place across the ocean. "I wish he'd hurry and come back," said Larry. "I miss him. He played catch with me."

Then one day Larry's parents got a sad phone call. Uncle George was lost. "We don't know where he is yet," said the man on the phone. "We'll call you back."

Every day they waited to hear about Uncle George. He was gone a l-o-n-g time. Finally, the special phone call came. "We found him!" the man said. "He's OK!"

Larry jumped up and down. "Uncle George is coming home!" he shouted. The next day the whole family went to the airport to meet Uncle George. They hugged. They laughed. They cried happy tears. "God, thanks so much. You've brought us back together again," prayed Larry. Perhaps Larry and his family felt like Joseph and his family in the Bible story.

Questions
1. Who moved away? (Uncle George)
2. Who brought the family back together again? (God)

Activities
1. Talk on a pretend phone.
2. Color a picture and send it to a relative or friend in a faraway place.

Prayer
Dear God, I know that you care about each one in my family. Thank you for watching over us when we're apart. Amen.

A GROWING FAMILY
Exodus 1:1-14; Exodus 2:23, 24

Call to me in times of trouble. I will save you. *Psalm 50:15*

When a man and woman get married and have babies, they become a family. After many years, the babies grow up to have families, too. _____ , this is how cities and countries grow.

A very long time ago, Jacob's family started with twelve baby boys who grew up and had babies. That kept happening year after year until there were about two million people! The two million men, women, and children were Israelites, but they lived in Egypt. They didn't live in their own place. (It would be like our family living in a country far away from us.)

The king of Egypt got worried. "I'm afraid all these people will fight us and take over our land," he said. "Let's do something to make sure that won't happen." So the Israelites became slaves in Egypt. They had to work very hard in the hot sun. The Israelites cried to God for help. They didn't know it then, but God planned to save them and get them out of Egypt.

Questions
1. How many sons did Jacob have? (Twelve)
2. How many Israelite people lived in Egypt? (About two million)
3. What did the king do to the Israelites? (Made them work very hard and beat them.)

Activities
1. Count to twelve.
2. Count as high as you can. (Two million is more than you and I can count.)

Prayer
Dear God, you say we can call to you when we're in trouble and you will help us. Help me to remember your promise when I'm in trouble. Amen.

JOINING GOD'S TEAM
Exodus 2:11; Acts 7:21-23

It was by faith that Moses, when he grew up, . . .
chose to suffer with God's people. *Hebrews 11:24, 25*

_____ , how old are you? Moses was about your age when the king's daughter adopted him. She took care of him and loved him as he grew up. Moses was different from the other children in the palace. He was a Hebrew.

One day when Moses was growing up, he started thinking about his Hebrew relatives. He wondered how they lived and if they were happy. So he went to see them in the hot fields where they worked. What he saw made him sad. He saw how hard they worked and how badly they were treated.

Moses made up his mind to be known as a Hebrew. In the king's house, he had lots of money and many things, but he gave that up to join the "team" of his Hebrew relatives and friends. Moses decided to join God's team.

Questions
1. Who adopted Moses? (The king's daughter)
2. What did Moses see that made him feel sad? (His relatives being badly treated)
3. What did Moses decide to do? (Be known as a Hebrew)

Activity
Name the positions of the different players on a baseball team. (Pitcher, catcher, shortstop, etc.) The players on a team work to help each other. When we join God's team, we are on his side.

Prayer
Dear God, Moses decided to join your team and help the Hebrew people. I want to join your team also. I want to do what makes you happy. Help me to do that. Amen.

RUNNING AND WAITING
Exodus 2:11-15; Acts 7:24-29

Wait for the Lord. He will make things right. *Proverbs 20:22*

_____ , listen and I'll tell you a story about why Moses moved away from Egypt.

Moses grew up in the king's house. He had everything he wanted. Then he decided to give it up so he could be known as a Hebrew. But Moses made a big mistake.

Walking in a field, Moses saw an Egyptian beating a Hebrew man. Moses got mad, killed the Egyptian, and hid his body in the sand. Moses thought no one saw him kill the Egyptian.

But the next day, someone asked Moses about it. Moses was afraid. So Moses ran away from Egypt, from the king, and from the people he wanted to help. He ran far away. When he finally stopped running, he sat down by a well to rest.

God had a plan for Moses to help the Hebrews get out of Egypt, but it wasn't the right time yet. God promises to help make things right, but sometimes we have to wait.

Questions
1. What did Moses decide to do? (Help the Hebrew people.)
2. After Moses made a mistake, what did he do? (He ran away.)
3. Was it the right time for Moses to help the people? (No)

Activities
1. Name some times when you or your child might have to wait. (Ideas: in line at the store, for guests to eat dinner, to go on vacation, for baby sister or brother to come)
2. Draw a picture of someone waiting.

Prayer
Dear God, would you please help me to learn to wait patiently for your help? Thank you. Amen.

HELPING OTHERS
Exodus 2:15-20

Share with God's people who need help. *Romans 12:13*

_____ , who ran away from Egypt? Yes, Moses did. He ran a long way and he was tired, so he sat down by a well to rest.

He had just closed his eyes when he heard laughter. The sound of voices made him open his eyes and turn. He saw 1, 2, 3, 4, 5, 6, 7 girls.

"Who are these young women?" he wondered. "What are they doing?" At just that moment some "big bully" shepherds pushed the girls away from the well. No one noticed Moses sitting on the rock. He surprised everyone when he rushed over to help. "Leave these women alone!" said Moses.

The seven girls were sisters. When they returned home, their father asked, "How did you finish watering the flocks so quickly today?"

"A man chased the shepherds away and then helped us water the animals," they said.

"I want to thank him," said their father, Jethro. "Go and invite him to eat dinner with us."

Moses helped the sisters when they had trouble with the shepherds. Like Moses, you and I can decide to help others when they are having trouble.

Questions
1. What were the seven women doing? (Getting water for their sheep.)
2. Who helped them? (Moses)

Activities
1. Count to seven.
2. Name ways you might help others.

Prayer
Dear God, please help me to be a helper like Moses. Amen.

GOD SEES EVERYONE
Exodus 2:16-25

He sees every person. From his throne he watches everyone.
Psalm 33:13, 14

"Thank you, young man, for helping my seven daughters today at the well," said the man named Jethro. "When the selfish shepherds bother my girls, it takes them a long time to get water. Today was different. We want to make you dinner to say thank you."

Soon Jethro invited Moses to stay and eat many meals with them. Moses helped with the sheep. He married one of the seven sisters, and they had a baby boy.

Moses was busy with his new family. But back in Egypt, God's people still worked very hard. They cried to God for help. Moses wanted to help them, but now he lived in a faraway place. How could he help them?

_____ , did God care about these people in Egypt who prayed to him? Yes, he did. He had a plan to get them out of Egypt, and Moses was going to be part of that plan.

Questions
1. Who had seven daughters? (The man named Jethro)
2. Who helped the sisters with their sheep? (Moses)
3. Did God care about his hurting people in Egypt? (Yes)

Activities
1. Count to seven.
2. Invite someone to dinner or lunch.

Prayer
Dear God, you cared about Jethro and his family. You cared about Moses. You cared about your people in Egypt. You care about my family and me, too, and I'm glad. Amen.

Note to parents/teachers
Explain that God can be in two places at the same time. Two people can pray to him at the same time and he hears both of them. God can help more than one person at a time. God is *omnipresent*. That means he can be with all people and in all places at the same time. Read the verses from Psalm 33:13, 14.

MOSES IS AFRAID
Exodus 3:1-13

The Lord your God will be with you everywhere you go. *Joshua 1:9*

"Moses, I've heard the prayers of my people in Egypt. I know the Egyptians hurt them. I know they are poor. I want to get them away from there and take them to a good land. I promised them this land years ago," said God. "I have a plan. I want you to get them out."

"But God, I can't do that," said Moses. "I'm not a leader. I don't know what to do. I'm afraid."

"Don't worry," said God. "I'll be with you. You will lead my people out. Then you and the people will come back here to this mountain where we are now."

Moses thought he couldn't do the job God asked him to do. It looked too hard. _____ , sometimes you and I might think we can't do what God wants us to do, either. But God promises to be with us always. He will help us have courage to do what we need to do.

Questions
1. Who heard the prayers of the hurting people in Egypt? (God)
2. What did God want Moses to do? (Get the people out of Egypt)
3. How did Moses answer God? ("I can't do it. I'm afraid.")
4. What did God tell Moses? ("I will be with you.")

Activities
1. Name some things you might think you just cannot do.
2. Say the verse together.

Prayer
Dear God, I need your help. Sometimes it's hard for me to share, wait, or obey. But I know you will always help me. Thanks. Amen.

Note to parents/teachers
This might be a good time to briefly share one of your own struggles. This honesty may encourage your child that he is not alone with his feelings of fear or reluctance. (Ideas: I thought it was hard to go to a new job, move to a new house, go to the hospital, go to work when very tired.) When a task seems hard, we can remember that God is with us. He will take care of us.

STILL WORRIED
Exodus 3:13 — 4:5

Obey me . . . and I will be your God. Jeremiah 11:4

"I will be with you," promised God. But Moses was still worried. "What if the people want to know who told me to come and take them out of Egypt?" Moses asked.

"Tell them that the God of their relatives Abraham, Isaac, and Jacob told you to come," answered God. "Tell them I haven't forgotten them."

"What if they don't believe me?" asked Moses. He was still worried.

"OK, Moses, I see you're still worried," said God. "I'm going to show you something so you'll remember that you can trust me to take care of you. See that stick in your hand. Throw it on the ground."

Moses threw it down. Quickly he jumped away when he saw a snake and not a stick. Then God said, "Moses, reach out and grab the snake by the tail." Moses did, and the snake became a stick again.

_____ , God is powerful. He can do anything. God wanted Moses to believe that he could help him do this big job. God wants us to believe that he can help us each day, too.

Questions
1. Who was still worried? (Moses)
2. Who promised to help Moses get the people out of Egypt? (God)

Activity
Name the three men who were relatives of the people. (Abraham, Isaac, Jacob)

Prayer
Dear God, you talked to Moses when he was scared. You helped him understand, and then he obeyed. Please help me to understand and obey you even when I'm scared. Amen.

I CAN'T DO IT!
Exodus 3:12; 4:15

I will not be afraid because the Lord is with me. *Psalm 118:6*

Davey tried to tie his shoes. "I can't do it," he cried. He tried to button his coat. "I can't do it," he said again.

"Come on, Davey," said Mom. "We're going to preschool today."

"I can't do it" he yelled. "I can't go to class by myself." Mom took Davey's hand and walked to the car. She sang him a song. But he cried so loud he couldn't hear the words. "I can't do it. I can't," he screamed.

Moses said, "I can't do it," when God asked him to do a special job. Moses was afraid — just like Davey. But God said, "Moses, I'll be with you." In the Bible, God tells all of us, "Don't be afraid. I will be with you."

_____ , remember when Moses decided to believe God. Do you think Davey will decide to believe that God is with him? Do you think Davey will stop crying?

Questions
1. Who cried "I can't do it!"? (Davey)
2. Where were Davey and his mom going? (To preschool)
3. What does God say in the Bible? ("Don't be afraid. I will be with you.")

Activities
1. Write the verse above on a sheet of paper. Have your child color the page. Display it in his room.
2. Say Psalm 118:6 together.

Prayer
Dear God, I won't worry when I have to try something new, because I know you're with me.

WORKING TOGETHER
Exodus 4:18-23

Then he sent his servant Moses, and Aaron, whom he had chosen.
Psalm 105:26

_____ , we usually travel in our car when we want to go somewhere, don't we? Moses and his family went to Egypt. God wanted Moses to help the hurting people there. But Moses didn't drive a car; there were no cars. His wife and two sons rode a donkey while Moses walked.

God promised to help Moses. "When you get to Egypt, I'll give you the power to do very special things. Show these special things to the king of Egypt," said God.

While Moses was on this trip, God talked to Moses' brother, Aaron. "Moses is coming to Egypt. Go meet him," said God. So Moses and Aaron met each other at Mount Sinai. Then Moses told Aaron all that God had said to him. And Aaron agreed he would help Moses in Egypt.

When they came to Egypt, God told Moses the words to say, and Moses told them to Aaron. Then Aaron talked to the hurting Israelite people. The people watched as Moses showed them God's power with his walking stick. They believed that God had heard their prayers for help. They bowed down and thanked God for remembering them in their trouble.

Questions
1. Who told Moses what to say? (God)
2. Who talked to the people? (Aaron)
3. Did the people believe that God was going to help them? (Yes)

Activity
Take a pretend walking trip. Name the things you would take to camp out on the way.

Prayer
Dear God, Moses and Aaron talked to the hurting people in Egypt. The people believed and worshiped you. I believe and worship you today, too. Amen.

IT'S NOT WORKING!
Exodus 5:22 — 6:9

I am the Lord . . . God All-Powerful. Exodus 6:2, 3

_____ , have you ever been told to do something and you didn't know why? Maybe you didn't understand why Mom told you to take a nap. Why take a nap when you don't feel tired? Yet mom knew you'd be tired and grouchy when grandma visited if you didn't rest. Or perhaps Dad told you to wear a jacket to the ball game. "I'm not cold," you said. But Dad knew the sun would go down and it would turn cold. Mom and Dad knew what was best.

Moses wondered why God told him to talk to the king of Egypt. It only made the king angry. It didn't work to talk to him. The king still said no to letting the people leave Egypt.

"God, why did you send me here?" asked Moses. "The king hurts the people even more since Aaron and I came. Now the people won't even listen to us."

"Moses, it may seem like it's not working," said God. "But you watch. You'll see how great I am. The king will change his mind. I am God. I can do anything. Believe me."

Questions
1. Who talked to the king? (Moses and Aaron)
2. Did the king decide to let the people go? (No, not yet)
3. Who said, "It seems like it's not working. But watch me. I can do anything"? (God)

Activity
Draw a picture of the king and a picture of Moses.

Prayer
Dear God, Moses didn't understand exactly what you were doing. Sometimes I don't understand what is best, either. But I know you are great. You do what works best for me. Thanks. Amen.

HAVING FAITH
Hebrews 11:23-29

Faith means being sure of the things we hope for. Hebrews 11:1

_____ , do you know anyone who lives across the ocean? Patrick did. He had a friend who lived in a faraway country. His friend liked to read storybooks. He wanted to read about Jesus. But the leaders of his country wouldn't let him. Patrick's friend wanted to go to Sunday school. But his country's leaders wouldn't let him do that, either.

So Patrick's friend decided to pray about his problem. "Dear God, you know what is happening here in my country," he prayed. "They keep me from going to Sunday school and reading stories about your Son, Jesus. I have faith that one day you will make my wish come true. I believe you when you say that you are with me always. Please help the leaders to change their minds."

Patrick's friend had faith just like Moses did. Moses believed that one day the mean king of Egypt would let the people go. And Patrick's friend believed that one day he would be able to read about Jesus and go to Sunday school. God is glad when we have faith.

Questions
1. Who prayed to God about his wish? (Patrick's friend)
2. What did Patrick's friend want to do? (Read stories about Jesus and go to Sunday school)

Activities
1. Read a picture book.
2. Write to a friend who lives far away.

Prayer
Dear God, I believe that you hear both my prayer and the prayer of those children who live far away. I have faith that you will help both of us. Amen.

"NO" CHANGED TO "GO"
Exodus 7:14 — 11:3; 12:31-33

Go and worship the Lord.
Exodus 12:31

"No, no, no!" yelled the king of Egypt.

"God says you should let his people go," said Moses.

"God? Who is God?" said the king. "I don't have to listen to anyone named God."

"Then God says the water in the river will turn to blood." And it did. Everywhere in Egypt, except where the Israelites were living, all the water in the river turned to blood. No one in Egypt, not even the king, had any water to drink.

But the king still would not let God's people go. So God sent gobs of frogs to jump all over. Then the king said the people could go.

But the next day he changed his mind. This time God sent swarms of tiny flying bugs. God also had to send swarms of flies, then sicknesses, then hail, then locusts, then darkness that lasted three days. Every time the king said the people could go, but he always changed his mind.

Finally God send an angel over Egypt. The oldest son in every Egyptian family died, even the son of the king.

"Go! Go!" the king said to Moses then. "Take your people and leave."

Questions
1. Who finally said "Go" instead of "No"? (The king)
2. What happened when the king said no? (God sent problems to the Egyptians.)
3. What kinds of animals did God send to cause problems for the Egyptians? (Frogs, tiny flying bugs, flies, and locusts)

Activity
Write the words "No" and "Go" on a sheet of paper. These words rhyme, but have different first letters. Trace over the letters with a crayon or marker.

Prayer
Dear God, Moses obeyed you even when the king would not. Help me to obey you even if others don't. Amen.

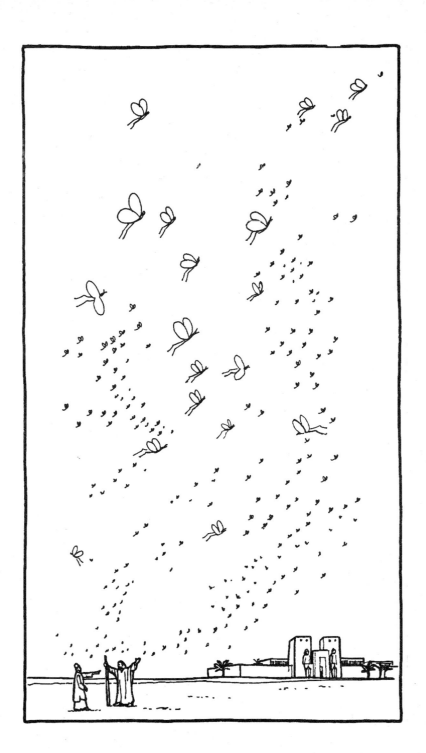

SOUNDS LIKE THUNDER
Exodus 14:5-15

Don't be afraid! Stand still and see the Lord save you today.
Exodus 14:13

_____ , remember when the king finally told Moses to take the people and go? Moses did just that. But then the king changed his mind again. "Why did I let those people go?" he yelled. "They worked for me. Now they're gone. Let's go get them back."

So the king called together all the soldiers in his huge army. "Get your chariots ready," he shouted. "We're going after the Israelites." The horses pulling the chariots raced down the dirt road, making a loud noise that sounded like thunder.

"Look! They're after us!" cried the people. "We have to get across the Red Sea or they'll catch us!" They prayed for help.

"Don't be afraid!" said Moses. "God has a surprise plan. He'll help us get across the water. Let's stay calm and watch God do it."

Questions
1. Who changed his mind again? (The king of Egypt)
2. Who came after the Israelite people? (The king and his army)
3. Who was afraid? (The Israelite people)
4. What did Moses say? ("Don't be afraid. God has a plan.")

Activities
1. Pretend you are in a chariot, directing the horses on the road.
2. Name times when you might feel afraid. (Ideas: when you're alone, in a storm, at nighttime, with a new baby-sitter.)

Prayer
Dear God, Moses told the people not to worry. But it looked very scary to the people. Sometimes things look scary to me, too. That's when I need your help. Amen.

WE'RE THIRSTY!
Exodus 15:22-27

I asked the Lord for help, and he answered me. *Psalm 34:4*

_____, have you ever been thirsty? What did you need to help your thirsty throat? You needed a drink of water, didn't you? After God helped the Hebrews cross the Red Sea, Moses led them toward their new home. They had walked for three long days without water. "We're tired and thirsty," they said. So Moses stopped at a desert place called Marah, where there was water to drink. Finally they would get a drink.

But as soon as the people gulped the water, they spit it out. "Ugh!" they shouted. "We can't drink this stuff. It tastes terrible." Then Moses prayed to God for help.

"See that piece of wood, Moses?" asked God. "Pull it out of the ground and throw it in the water." Moses did what God said to do. Then he took a sip of water.

"It tastes great," Moses said. "God helped us again."

God wanted the Israelite people to stop their grouchy grumbling and trust him. "Listen to me and believe me when I say that I'll take care of you," said God. God takes care of us, too. We can trust him to give us what we need.

Questions
1. Who was thirsty? (Moses and the people)
2. How long did the people walk? (Three days)
3. What was wrong with the water at Marah? (It tasted bad.)

Activity
Enjoy a cup of cool, refreshing water together.

Prayer
Dear God, I could get sick without water to drink. Thanks for making water for me to drink and for taking care of me. Amen.

QUAIL FOR DINNER
Exodus 16:1-13

When they asked, he brought them quail. He filled them with
bread from heaven. *Psalm 105:40*

"Hey, Moses, you want us
to starve to death?" grumbled
the people. "Maybe we should
have stayed in Egypt. At least
we had meat to eat there."

Moses and Aaron called all
the people together. "You think
you're grumbling and com-
plaining to us, but you're really
being grouchy to God," said
Moses. "Why do you forget so
quickly? Remember when God
helped you get away from the
mean king of Egypt. He'll help us now, too. Tomorrow you'll see
again how great our God is."

The next evening God sent birds called quail into the camp-
ground. The quail tasted a little bit like a yummy chicken supper.
_____ , do you like to eat chicken for dinner?

God didn't forget his people. Even though they had complained, God gave them good food to eat. God provided for Moses
and the people. He will take care of us, too.

Questions
1. Who were the people really grumbling to? (God)
2. What did God send for them to eat for dinner? (Quail)
3. Did God forget his people? (No)

Activities
1. Have your child pretend to make and serve you a good chicken
   dinner.
2. Ask your child what his favorite meal is. Plan to have this meal
   within the next week.

Prayer
Dear God, you took care of the people. I know you'll take care of
me, too. I'm thankful. Amen.

54

WHAT'S FOR BREAKFAST?
Exodus 16:21-31

A greedy person causes trouble. But the one who trusts the Lord will succeed. *Proverbs 28:25*

_____ , what did you eat for breakfast this morning? (Pause for answer.) That sounds good. God sent a good breakfast each morning for the Israelite people. A special food called "manna" came down from the sky like rain. It looked like little seeds and tasted like crackers with honey. It could be eaten plain, baked into bread, or boiled with water to make cereal.

God sent just enough manna for each day. The people were to take only what they needed. Some of the people tried to take more, but that wasn't a good idea, because the manna spoiled and smelled bad and then they couldn't eat it. Moses told the people not to worry about the next morning's breakfast. God would take care of them. He will take care of us, too.

Questions
1. Who made breakfast each morning for the Israelite people? (God)
2. What was the breakfast food called? (Manna)
3. What was the manna like? (Little seeds that tasted sweet)

Activities
1. Name your favorite breakfast food.
2. Draw a picture of the "manna" food.

Prayer
Dear God, help me to trust you for everything I need. I know you care about me and will take care of my needs. Amen.

THE BIG DRINKING FOUNTAIN
Exodus 17:1-7

God split the rock, and water flowed out.
It ran like a river through the desert.
Psalm 105:41

Moses had a hard job to do. He was the teacher and leader of about two million people! Sometimes the people laughed. Sometimes they complained.

_____ , sometimes it's a hard job for me to be your teacher and leader. Little children are happy at times and grouchy other times. I care about you all the time. Moses cared about the people, too.

Moses and the people walked a long way. They couldn't find any water. "Give us a drink," said the people. "We need water! Even our animals are thirsty."

Moses talked to God. "These people are mad at me, Lord. What am I going to do?"

"Take some grandpas with you and walk on ahead of the others," said God. "Take the same stick you used when the waters of the Red Sea split. Hit that big rock over there with your stick." Moses did just what God said to do. The grandpas watched. Water came out of the rock like a big drinking fountain. Again God took care of the people.

Questions
1. Why were the people mad at Moses? (They were thirsty and had no water.)
2. What did God tell Moses to do? (Hit the rock. Water would come out.)
3. Did Moses obey God? (Yes)

Activity
Name some times when you might be thirsty. (Ideas: when you take a long walk, when you play hard, when you are sick with a fever, when you eat crackers.)

Prayer
Dear God, you cared about the people even when they were grouchy. Moses cared, too. And Mom and Dad care about me even when I'm grouchy. I'm glad. Thank you. Amen.

VISITING MOSES
Exodus 18:1-8

I will praise you, Lord, with all my heart. I will tell all the miracles you have done. Psalm 9:1

While Moses was on the long trip with the Israelite people, his family stayed with Grandpa Jethro. There were no telephones in those days, so news traveled very slowly. It took many weeks for Moses' wife, two sons, and Jethro to find out how Moses was doing. Finally Jethro heard that God had saved all the people from the Egyptian king.

"This is great news about Moses. Let's take a trip to go see him," said Jethro. While they traveled, Jethro sent a letter to Moses. The letter said, "Dear Moses, I'm bringing your wife and two sons for a visit. See you soon. Love, Jethro."

Moses was happy to see his family. He ran to meet them on the road. "God saved us from the king and his army," he said. "We've had lots of problems. But God helped us every time we needed help."

Questions
1. How many children did Moses have? (Two sons)
2. Who came to see Moses? (Jethro, Moses' wife, and his two sons)

Activity
Name your grandpas (example: Grandpa George is Mom's daddy; Grandpa Smith is Daddy's father.) Fill in the blanks:

_____ loves Grandpa _____ .
_____ loves Grandpa _____ .

Prayer
Dear God, Moses said that it was you who helped him lead the people out of Egypt. Just like Moses, I know that every good thing that happens to me is a gift from you. I will tell my friends about how you help me and take care of me. Thank you. Amen.

A THANK-YOU PARTY
Exodus 18:9-12

Tell the greatness of the Lord with me. Let us praise
his name together. *Psalm 34:3*

_____ , what is your grandpa's name?

Moses had two sons, and their grandpa's name was Jethro. When Jethro came to visit, Moses told him about how the Red Sea opened up and the people walked through on dry ground. Moses told Jethro about the water that came out of the rock like a drinking fountain and about the manna that came out of the sky. "God has done lots of good things for us," said Moses.

"Praise the Lord," Jethro said. "I know God is bigger and greater than anyone else. I want to thank God. I want to praise God and worship him."

Then Moses, Jethro, and the leaders of the people all got together to praise God. They ate dinner together. They had a thank-you party.

Questions
1. Who was Grandpa Jethro? (Moses' sons' grandpa)
2. What did Jethro say when Moses told him about how God helped them? (Praise the Lord. God is greater than anyone else.)
3. Who ate together at the thank-you party? (Moses, Jethro, and the leaders)

Activities
1. Name some ways God has helped you.
2. Plan a meal together. Call it a thank-you party. Write several thank-you notes to God. Tie each one to a balloon and attach the balloon at each place setting.

Prayer
Dear God, you are greater than anyone. You help me. Thank you.

STANDING IN LINE
Exodus 18:13-20

A wise person listens to advice. Proverbs 12:15

_____ , has Grandpa or Grandma ever stayed all night with you? Grandpa Jethro stayed all night with Moses. The next morning, Jethro saw many of the people standing around Moses. Moses didn't have time to eat or rest.

"What are all these people doing?" asked Jethro. "Why are you the only one who can talk to them? There isn't any time for you to do anything else. "

"They come to me for God's help with their problems," answered Moses.

"Moses, I don't think you're doing this the right way," said Jethro. "You're going to get too tired. And the people will get tired of waiting. You can't do this all by yourself. There's too much to do. I know you want to do God's work, but you need help from the other people. I have an idea. I think it will help you. Will you listen to my idea?"

Moses was an important man. Still, he didn't think he was too important to listen to other people's advice. Grandpa Jethro wanted to help Moses.

Questions
1. Who stood in line waiting to see Moses? (People who wanted help with their problems)
2. Who said Moses would get too tired? (Jethro)
3. Did Moses think he was too important to listen to Jethro? (No)

Activity
Draw a picture of all the people who came to see Moses.

Prayer
Dear God, help me to listen to someone who has an idea that will help me. I know that I don't always have all the answers. Amen.

GOOD IDEA!
Exodus 18:21-26

Two people are better than one. They get more done
by working together. *Ecclesiastes 4:9*

Jethro saw the long lines of people waiting to see Moses. Each
person standing in line wanted to talk about a problem. Moses was
so busy he didn't even have time to eat. "I think you're trying to
do too much, Moses," said Jethro. "You'll get too tired. I know you
want to do God's work. But you can't do everything. I have an
idea. Choose some God-loving men to help you. They should tell
the truth and want to help people. One man can be the helper to
ten people (or families). Then another man will help a hundred
people. And another will help a thousand people. These men will
take care of the everyday problems. You can help with the big,
hard problems. Sharing the work will be easier for you. Ask God if
he thinks this is a good idea."

_____ , Moses must have prayed about this idea, because
soon he did everything Jethro said. The good idea helped the people and Moses. They did things in order. This is called "being
organized." You and I can be "organized," too. Sometimes we
need each other's help.

Questions
1. Who had a good idea? (Jethro)
2. Did Jethro tell Moses to ask God about the idea? (Yes)

Activity
Name ways to be "organized" so the work will be easier. Ideas: (1)
One child put the forks and spoons on the table, and one child fill

the water glasses. (2) One
person pick up the blue toys,
one person pick up the red
toys. (3) Put blocks in a box,
books in another, dolls on a
special shelf.

Prayer
Dear God, help me listen to
others' good ideas. Help our
family to work together.

THE "ORGANIZED" CLASS
Exodus 18:13-26

But let everything be done in a way that is right and orderly.
1 Corinthians 14:40

The children ran to the classroom door. "Yeah, let's go!" they yelled. They shouted, pushed, and shoved. Elizabeth bumped into Eric and knocked him down. "Teacher, I want help," said Elizabeth. "No! Help me with my coat," said Steven. "No, help me first," cried Eric.

Mrs. Jones stood tall in the center of the room. "Wait a minute! We have a lot to do to get ready to go home. We need to be organized and help each other," she said. "Go back to your seats and sit down. I have an idea. All the boys and girls in the seats by the window get up quietly and put the toys back on the shelves. The children in the next row go over and get your coats and boots. Then bring them back to your seats. All the children in the back row put the books away. We'll have time to do everything if we do things nicely and in order."

_____ , God is happy when we do things in a way that is right and in order. We will be happier, too.

Questions
1. What was the teacher's name? (Mrs. Jones)
2. When did everything work better? (As each person helped; when things were done in order.)

Activities
1. Plan how to get ready for church. (Ideas: Get up when Mom calls you, make bed, get dressed, eat breakfast, brush teeth.)
2. Help each other make the beds.

Prayer
Dear God, help me to please you by doing things in a way that is right and in order. Amen.

UP AND DOWN THE MOUNTAIN
Exodus 19:1-7

Moses continued strong as if he could see the God that no one can see. *Hebrews 11:27*

_____ , have you ever tried to climb up a mountain? It's hard work. It takes strong legs and steady feet to walk between the rocks and cracks.

Moses must have been a strong man. He walked up a big mountain. On the mountain God called to Moses. "Remind the people that I led them out of Egypt," said God. "I gave them water, food, and a good leader. I brought them safely to this place. Now I'm asking that they obey me. I'll take care of them. They will be my special people."

So Moses walked back down the mountain. He called the leaders of the people to a meeting. Moses told them what God had said.

"We'll do everything God wants us to do," said the leaders. Then Moses climbed back up the mountain to tell God about the people's promise.

Moses cared about the people. He knew that God cared about the people, too, and wanted them to be happy and healthy. God planned to give Moses some special rules that would help the people live loving, good lives.

Questions
1. Who planned to give Moses some rules for happy living? (God)
2. Who walked up the big mountain? (Moses)

Activities
1. Pretend to climb a mountain together.
2. Find a picture of a mountain in the encyclopedia or a magazine.

Prayer
Dear God, Moses always listened to you and did what you said. I want to do what you say to do, too. Please help me. Amen.

GOD'S TEN SPECIAL RULES
Exodus 20:1-17

I thought about my life, and I decided to obey your rules.
Psalm 119:59

_____ , God wants us to be safe and happy. Long ago God told Moses about ten special rules that can help us live good and loving lives. These rules were important to the people then, and they are important to us today. Here is what God said:

1. Worship only me. Other gods cannot help you.
2. Let nothing be more important than knowing me.
3. Always say my name with loving care.
4. Work for six days. Rest and worship me on the seventh day.
5. Obey and honor your parents.
6. Don't kill anyone.
7. Be faithful to your husband or wife.
8. Never take anything that is not yours.
9. Always tell the truth about your friends and neighbors.
10. Don't want to take someone else's things.

Some people may say that these ten special rules aren't good anymore. That isn't true. These rules still make a lot of sense today. When people decide not to follow God's rules, their lives get mixed-up and sad. Usually they get into trouble. God gave these rules because he loves us very much. He wants us to be happy and safe.

Questions
1. Who was the first person to hear God's special rules? (Moses)
2. How many special rules did God give to Moses? (Ten)
3. Are these rules still good today? (Yes)

Activities
1. Count to ten.
2. Name one of God's special rules. (See list above.)

Prayer
Dear God, I've thought about it and I want to be a good, loving, happy person when I grow up. So I've decided to pay attention to your rules. I believe you love me. Please help me. Amen.

BROKEN STONES
Exodus 32:18-26

You must decide whom you will serve. Joshua 24:15

Moses stayed on the moun-
tain with God for forty days. God
wrote the rules with his finger on
two flat stones and gave them to
Moses. Moses carried the stones
back down the mountain. Then
he saw something that made him
feel sad and angry. The people
were singing, dancing, and praying to a statue of a golden calf.
Moses threw the stones down.
CRASH! BANG! They broke into little pieces. "Aaron, what are
you doing?" asked Moses. "How could you all forget your
promise to God?"

"You know how it is," said Aaron. "The people are always getting into trouble. I melted their gold jewelry and this gold calf just
showed up." Aaron didn't say that he had a part in the making of
the gold calf.

Then Moses stood in front of the people. "Anyone who wants
to follow God, come stand by me," he said. The people needed to
choose. Would they pray and sing to the true God? Or would they
still pray and sing to the golden calf? _____ , we have a
choice, too. Let's always choose God.

Questions
1. How long was Moses on the mountain with God? (Forty days)
2. Who wrote on the stones with his finger? (God)
3. What were the people's choices? (To pray and sing to the golden
   calf or to obey the true God)

Activity
Talk about choices. Name some choices you make each day. (Ideas:
which shirt to wear, which toy to play with, whether to do what
Mom says, whether to be kind to brother/sister)

Prayer
Dear God, help me to make good and right choices. Amen.

WHAT IS GOD LIKE?
Exodus 34:6-10

The Lord has great love and faithfulness. *Exodus 34:6*

"Mom," asked Jeremy, "what is God like? Is he like Superman?"

"No, not exactly," answered Mom.

"Is he like Daddy or Uncle Joe?" Jeremy asked. "They're very strong."

"Well, no, not exactly," said Jeremy's mom. "No one is just like God. Moses found out about God. God gave him those ten special rules and then said, "I am the Lord. I'm the one who has always been around — before anyone else. I'll help anyone who wants my help. I'm kind. I give people a chance to try again when they make a mistake. I don't get angry quickly. I have lots of love. It doesn't really matter to me if a person is tall or short, black or white, rich or poor.

"I do get sad when people act like they don't care about me. But I'm always ready to forgive. And I'm fair. I can't let people keep doing bad things without correcting or punishing them. I let people make their own decisions, though. And I like to do wonderful things for people. I want everyone to know who I am and what I'm like."

"I like God," said Jeremy. "You do, too, don't you, Mom?"

Questions
1. Who asked, "What is God like?" (Jeremy)
2. Who has lots of love? (God)
3. Is God like Superman? (No, there is no one like God.)

Activities
1. Name things you know about God.
2. Draw a picture of what you think God is like.

Prayer
Dear God, you are loving, kind, forgiving, fair, and good. Thank you for caring about me. Amen.

SHINY FACES, SHINY LIVES
Exodus 34:29-35

We all show the Lord's glory, and we are being changed
to be like him. *2 Corinthians 3:18*

"Look at Moses," whispered the people. "He looks different.
His face is shining like a light." Then the people hid. They were
afraid to look at Moses' shiny face.

"It's OK," said Moses. "You don't have to hide. Come over
beside me and I'll tell you what God told me." After Moses finished talking to the people, he put a covering over his face. Each
time Moses talked to God, he took the covering off. Then his face

got all shiny again. God is
light. When Moses was with
God it seemed that some of
God's light rubbed off on
Moses.

_____ , you and I
can talk to God in prayer.
We can spend time learning
and reading about God. We
can listen to what he says.
Our lives can get "shiny" or
glad when we spend time
with God. Moses listened to
God. He spent time with
God. We can do that, too.

Questions
1. Who whispered about Moses? (The people)
2. Whose face was shiny? (Moses)
3. Why was Moses' face shiny? (Because he spent time with God)

Activities
1. Name ways that we can spend time with God.
2. Turn a light off and on. Notice the difference the light makes in
   how you can see and play.

Prayer
Dear God, I believe in you. Please make my life "shiny" when I
spend time with you. Amen.

THE LONGEST DAY
Joshua 10:1-14

Truly the Lord was fighting for Israel! *Joshua 10:14*

Joshua became the leader of God's people after Moses. Joshua said, "Get ready! God's going to do some wonderful things for you." Joshua was right.

First, God pulled back the water in the river. When the people walked across into their new land, they didn't even get muddy. But their new city had tall walls around it. The gate was locked. So God made the walls fall down.

Then God did another miracle. The leaders of five cities got together to fight against Joshua. But Joshua said, "Don't be afraid! It'll be OK! God will help us win!"

God did help them. God made the sun stand still in the sky. The daytime lasted longer than ever before. It didn't get dark outside. That meant Joshua and his men could keep fighting until they won. Every other day the sun had come up in the morning and gone down at night. But this day was different. Everything stopped. The sun stayed in the blue sky for an extra long time.

_____ , God did three exciting and wonderful things for the people — miracles — just like Joshua said he would.

Questions
1. What is a "miracle"? (A very special and wonderful thing that God does)
2. How many "miracles" did God do for Joshua and the people? (Three)

Activity
Form a circle with your hands above your head. Pretend it is the sun that God made to stand still in the sky.

Prayer
Dear God, you helped Joshua. Please help me today, too. No one can help like you do. Amen.

PROMISES! PROMISES!
Joshua 24:22-27

We can trust God to do what he promised. *Hebrews 10:23*

"Andy!" called Mother. "Please run next door and give this stick of butter to Linda's mom. Then you can stay and play with Linda."

"OK, Mom," Andy said. "Don't worry. I'll do it." Andy ran across the yard to Linda's house. He saw Linda playing catch with Michael and quickly forgot about his promise. He put the butter stick on a rock and played catch until Mom called for dinner.

"Oh, no!" Andy said. He ran to the rock and found the butter had melted in the sun. He raced home. "I'm sorry, Mom," he cried. "I forgot to give the butter to Linda's mom. It melted."

Mom knew Andy was sorry. "Here's some more butter, Andy. Take it over to Linda's mom. Then come straight home." Andy learned a lesson that day: It is important to keep the promises you make. _____ , God always keeps his promises to us. He can help us keep our promises, too.

Questions
1. Who forgot his promise to his mom? (Andy)
2. Who never forgets his promises? (God)

Activities
1. Name a promise you'd like to keep. (Ideas: to brush teeth each day; to wash hands before eating; to pray for a friend)
2. Place a stick of butter in the sun. Watch what happens when it gets hot.

Prayer
Dear God, help me keep my promises. You promised to help me, so I know you will. Thanks. Amen.

JUDGE DEBORAH
Judges 3 — 5

I . . . will sing to the Lord. *Judges 5:3*

The people had promised they would love and serve God. But do you know what happened? They didn't keep the promise. They forgot about God. They prayed to a fake god. They were bad to their children. They lied to God and to each other. God was sad. He cared about them, but he didn't like the way they talked and acted.

_____ , God gave the people new leaders called "judges." Most judges were men. But there was a woman judge named Deborah.

While Deborah was judge, the people prayed to God. They needed God's help because a bad king had hurt them for twenty years. God heard the people's prayer. Judge Deborah helped lead the people's army, and they won the fight against the bad king.

Then Deborah sang a praise song to God. She thanked God for helping her to do a good job as judge.

Questions
1. Did the people forget the promise they had made? (Yes)
2. What were the new leaders called? (Judges)
3. What was the woman judge's name? (Deborah)

Activities
1. Sing "Thank him, thank him, all you little children" (a verse of "Praise Him, Praise Him").
2. Make up a thank-you song.

Prayer
Dear God, thank you for helping me when I ask you. Amen.

A SMALL ARMY WINS
Judges 6:7 — 7:24

When you are weak, then my power is made perfect in you.
2 Corinthians 12:9

"Lord God, help us," cried the people. "The Midianites are taking over our land."

So God sent an angel to a young man named Gideon. "Hello," said the angel. "The Lord is with you. You are a strong soldier."

"What do you mean?" asked Gideon. "If God is with us, then why are these Midianites hurting us? Maybe you're talking to the wrong guy, because I'm sure not very important or strong."

"You, Gideon, are going to fight against the Midianites. I'll help you. And you'll win," said God. So Gideon chose 32,000 army men. But God said, "You have too many men. Tell those who are afraid to go home." So 22,000 men left. But God said, "You still have too many men." Then Gideon gave the 10,000 men a test. Only 300 men passed. "Now you'll know you have won the fight because I helped you," said God. "You can't say you did it with a big army."

Sometimes we think we're not strong, important, or brave enough to do what God wants. But when God helps us, we can do whatever he asks us to do.

Questions
1. Whom did God ask to lead the fight against the Midianites? (Gideon)
2. How many men were left in the army at the end? (300)

Activity
Fill in the blank with your name: God helps _____ to be brave.

Prayer
Dear God, sometimes I'm not very brave. Would you please help me? Amen.

72

GROWING UP TO LOVE GOD
1 Samuel 1:9-11, 19-27; 3:1, 19-21

The Lord was with Samuel as he grew up. 1 Samuel 3:19

Hannah wanted a baby. "Dear God," she prayed, "please think about my problem. I want a baby boy so much, I can't stop crying. If you give me a son, I'll give him back to you. He'll work for you all his life." Hannah soon learned she would have a baby! She waited nine long months and gave birth to Samuel. "God is good," sang Hannah. "He gave me a son."

Each year Hannah and her husband traveled to the big worship tent. But the year Samuel was born, Hannah told Elkanah to go without her. "I'm going to wait until Samuel is a little older," she said. "Then I'll take him to the worship tent church to live with Eli, the priest. He will serve God all his life."

Hannah wanted to keep her promise to God. So she rocked and nursed Samuel. She loved him and taught him to obey. She talked and played with him. Perhaps she told him about her special promise. _____ , Samuel grew up to love God.

Questions
1. Who wanted a baby boy? (Hannah)
2. What did Hannah say to her husband when it was time to go to the temple? (I'm going to wait until Samuel is a little older.)
3. What promise did Hannah want to keep? (That Samuel would serve God)

Activities
1. Play a quiet game together with your child.
2. Hug your child and say, "I love you."

Prayer
Dear God, thank you that Hannah thought it was important to love, teach, and play with little Samuel. Thank you that my mom (dad, grandma, etc.) loves and plays with me, too. Amen.

GOD LIKES MUSIC
1 Samuel 2:1-10

Make music to the Lord with harps, with harps and the sound of singing. Psalm 98:5

_____ , it's fun to sing songs, isn't it? Joey likes to sing, too. Joey lives next door to Mrs. Watson. Mrs. Watson has a shiny black grand piano in her house. Some days Joey walks over and knocks on Mrs. Watson's door. "May I play the piano?" he asks.

"Sure," says Mrs. Watson. Then Joey sits down on the padded bench. He makes music by carefully touching the black and white keys. Joey likes to sing and play pretty music. Mrs. Watson smiles when she hears Joey's music.

God likes music, too. He likes hearing his children sing songs. Samuel's mother, Hannah, sang a sweet praise song to God. She was so thankful God gave her a son. She sang, "My heart is happy in the Lord. There is no other one like him. I praise his name."

Small or big people — young or old people — can play songs and sing to God. God made music. He loves to hear us sing to him.

Questions
1. What did Mrs. Watson have in her house? (Shiny black piano)
2. Who liked to play the piano? (Joey)
3. Who sang a praise song to God? (Hannah, Samuel's mother)

Activity
If you have a piano (or any other instrument), play and sing together with your child.

Prayer
Dear God, you made my voice to sing. Thank you. I will sing a song to you. You have done wonderful things. Amen.

GOD'S LITTLE HELPER
1 Samuel 2:11, 18-21, 26

Serve the Lord with all your heart. *Romans 12:11*

_____ , are you a helper? When you do something nice for your brother (sister, friend) or when you obey Mom and Dad, you are being God's good helper. Little Samuel was God's helper. He learned and worked with Eli the priest in the worship tent.

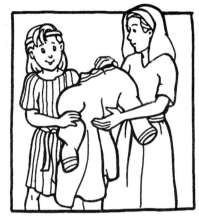

One day when Samuel was helping, he saw two people walking up the path. "It's my mom and dad!" Samuel said. He clapped his hands with joy.

Samuel's mother, Hannah, ran to hug Samuel. She handed him a package. Samuel opened the present and inside he found a nice warm coat, just his size. "I made it for you, Samuel," said Hannah. "Every time you wear it remember that Dad and I love you lots. I know you're growing up, so each year I'll make you a new one."

Samuel was God's little helper. He grew up to be God's big helper. We can be God's helpers, too.

Questions
1. What was in the package Samuel's mother gave him? (A nice warm coat just his size)
2. Who was God's helper? (Samuel)

Activities
1. Name ways that Samuel may have helped Eli in the worship tent? (Ideas: sweeping the floor, taking out the trash, greeting people, putting oil in the lamps)
2. Name ways you might help Mom and Dad.
3. Draw a picture of yourself helping a friend or family member.

Prayer
Dear God, please help me to be your good helper. Amen.

LOVING GOD
1 Samuel 15:1-34

I want faithful love more than I want animal sacrifices.
Hosea 6:6

"We want a king!" said the people. God had always been the people's leader. But now they wanted a king, so God let them have their way. Samuel helped God get the new king ready.

King Saul was tall, handsome, and strong. "God will help you," said Samuel. "Listen and do what he says." At first Saul listened to God. But then Saul decided he didn't need God.

Once, Saul had to fight against the king of another country. "I'll help you and you'll win," said God. "But don't bring any animals or people from the other country back with you."

Afterwards, Saul said to Samuel, "I did everything God asked me to do."

"How come I hear cows mooing and sheep going 'baa-baa'?" asked Samuel.

"It was the soldiers' idea," said Saul. "We thought we'd give the animals to God as a gift offering."

"Oh, Saul, God doesn't want these animal gifts," said Samuel. "He wants your love. He wants you to believe him and do what he says. That is more important than anything else."

_____ , God wants us to love and believe him, too. It's more important that anything else.

Questions
1. Who was strong, handsome, and strong? (King Saul)
2. What animal sounds did Samuel hear? (Cows mooing and sheep going "baa-baa")
3. What does God want from us more than anything else? (To love and believe God)

Activities
1. Make the sounds of a cow and a sheep.
2. Draw a picture of a cow and a picture of a sheep.

Prayer
Dear God, although I want to give you gifts of my time and money, I want to love and believe more than anything else. Help me. Amen.

HARD TIMES
1 Samuel 23 — 24, 26; 2 Samuel 1:1-27

Every good promise that the Lord your God made has come true.
Joshua 23:15

God promised to help David. And God did just what he said he would do. God kept David safe even when King Saul tried to hurt him. Jealous King Saul chased David all over the country.

It was a hard time for David. He ran from place to place. He hid in caves. He got tired. He got lonely.

Two times David and his soldiers could have hurt King Saul. They didn't, because David knew God didn't want him to hurt Saul. Finally, David and his followers moved far away from King Saul. Then Saul stopped chasing him.

One day a man ran to David. "Saul and Jonathan are dead," he shouted. The man thought David would be happy. But the news made David sad. Jonathan was David's friend. He loved him. Now both King Saul and Jonathan were gone. During all these sad and hard times, God helped David.

_____ , God kept his promise to David. He'll keep his promises to us, too.

Questions
1. Who helped David when King Saul chased him? (God)
2. Did David hurt King Saul? (No)

Activities
1. Make a promise to your child today. (Ideas: We'll take a walk together; I'll read you a story; we'll play a game together; I'll call you from work.)
2. Keep the promise.

Prayer
Dear God, thanks for promising to take care of me. I believe you'll keep your promise. Amen.

SHOWING KINDNESS
2 Samuel 9:1-13

Be kind. *Ephesians 4:32*

Jonathan was David's friend. _____ , do you think David called him Jon? Maybe. Even after many years, David and Jonathan stayed friends. Jonathan had a son named Mephibosheth (muh-FIB-oh-sheth). He was lame; something was wrong with his feet.

One day, David asked Jonathan's son to come visit him. Servants carried Mephibosheth into the room. When Mephibosheth saw King David, he bowed down.

David said, "Don't be afraid of me because I'm your king. Your father and I were good friends. I promised him I would be kind to his family. You're his family. I want to give you some land

to build a house. You're always welcome to eat dinner with me here at my house."

Mephibosheth bowed again. "You're very kind to me," he said. "Thank you."

David kept the promise he made to Jonathan. He showed kindness to Mephibosheth and all his family and helpers. We can learn to be kind to our friends, too.

Questions
1. Who was Mephibosheth's father? (Jonathan)
2. Who was kind to Mephibosheth? (King David)

Activities
1. Say "Mephibosheth" together.
2. Do something kind. (Ideas: Share a toy; smile at a neighbor; say nice words to your teacher; be a helper to Mom or Dad.)

Prayer
Dear God, King David was kind. Help me to be kind to my friends. Amen.

NATHAN'S STORY
2 Samuel 12:1-13

God, you will not reject a heart that is . . . sorry for its sin.
Psalm 51:17

God sent a man named Nathan to tell David a story:

"Once," said Nathan, "there was a very rich man who had lots of money, a big house, many animals, and all the food and clothes he wanted. He lived next to a man who had just one lamb.

"One day a visitor came to the rich man's house. He was hungry. But the rich man didn't share his own food. Instead, he took the poor man's only lamb."

David said, "The rich man is wrong! He must pay the poor man back."

"David, you are just like that man!" Nathan said. "You took what was not yours, and you thought no one saw you do it!"

"Oh, God," prayed David. "I've done wrong. I'm sorry. Make my heart feel glad again."

Nathan said, "God knows you're sorry. He has taken your sins away, David. He will forget what you did."

When you and I do something we shouldn't do, we can always talk to God about it, just like David did. God loves us. He will forgive us and forget about what we did.

Questions
1. Who was sorry for the wrong things that he did? (David)
2. Did God forgive and forget the wrong David did? (Yes)

Activity
Draw a picture of Nathan and David.

Prayer
Dear God, I'm sorry when I don't do what is right. Thanks for forgiving and forgetting about it. Help me to make the right choice the next time I think about doing wrong. Amen.

BLOW THE TRUMPET!
1 Kings 1:1-52

The Lord has given me many sons. And from those sons he has chosen Solomon. Solomon will be the new king.
1 Chronicles 28:5

_____ , King David had many sons. Solomon was one of the youngest. God told David that Solomon would be the next king.

Solomon's older brother, Adonijah, made up his mind to be king. He didn't ask what God wanted. He just said, "I will be king." He talked many people into following him. He didn't tell his father, David. And he didn't tell his brother Solomon about his plans.

When David heard that Adonijah tried to make himself king, he said, "No way! This isn't right. God said Solomon will be the next king. Let's blow the trumpet to tell everyone. Solomon is king! Shout the news!"

David knew Adonijah wasn't the right leader for the people. God's plan was for Solomon to be the next king. David decided to do what God wanted.

Questions
1. Who was going to be the next king? (Solomon)
2. Who wanted to be king, but didn't ask God? (Adonijah)
3. Were Solomon and Adonijah brothers? (Yes)

Activities
1. Pretend to blow a trumpet.
2. Draw a picture of a king's crown.

Prayer
Dear God, help me, like King David, to listen and obey your words and plan. Amen.

SOLOMON'S SCHOOL
1 Kings 4:29-34; 1 Kings 10:1-13;
Proverbs 30:24-31

God gave great wisdom to Solomon.
1 Kings 4:29

_____ , do you remember the name of the wise king? Yes, his name was Solomon. Solomon was the wisest man in the whole world. He wrote many stories, poems, and songs. He taught about plants and trees and all kinds of animals. People came from many different countries to go to Solomon's special school. They wanted to learn from the wisest man in the world.

One day an important queen traveled to see Solomon. The queen of Sheba brought many servants with her. It was a long trip by camel. But she wanted to know if Solomon was really as smart as everyone said he was.

The queen of Sheba asked Solomon lots of hard questions. Solomon answered every one. "You have a great God," said the queen of Sheba. "He has given you much wisdom."

Solomon wrote three books in the Bible. Those three books are Ecclesiastes, Song of Solomon, and most of the Proverbs. We can share some of Solomon's wisdom by reading what he wrote.

Questions
1. Who was the wisest man in the world? (Solomon)
2. What did Solomon teach about? (Plants, trees, and animals)
3. Who traveled to Solomon's school to ask some hard questions? (The queen of Sheba)
4. Who gave Solomon the wisdom he needed to answer the hard questions? (God)

Activities
1. Collect leaves from trees and bushes. How are they different? How are they the same?
2. Draw a picture of Solomon teaching a class.

Prayer
Dear God, you made the little ant and the big lion. You gave Solomon wisdom to know about a lot of things. Help me to learn from some of Solomon's wise words in the Bible. Amen.

GOD MADE IT RAIN
1 Kings 18:25-45

Then Elijah prayed again. And the rain came down from the sky.
James 5:18

King Ahab did not love God. And when Elijah told Ahab that there would be no rain for a long time, the news made King Ahab mad. He said it was all Elijah's fault.

But it wasn't Elijah's fault. Ahab and his family had made all the trouble. They ignored God and prayed to a statue named Baal. They asked Baal to send rain. But Baal couldn't hear them praying because he wasn't real. It did not rain.

Then God's friend and helper, Elijah, prayed for rain. There had been no rain clouds in the sky for a long time. When Elijah saw the first tiny cloud, he believed God had answered his prayer. Soon there were lots of clouds! And then it rained hard! Elijah said, "You have proved to the people that you are the one true God. You are powerful."

_____ , we love and pray to the same God that Elijah did. Our God is strong. He can do anything.

Questions
1. Who was the king who didn't love God? (Ahab)
2. Was Ahab mad at Elijah? (Yes)
3. Was it Elijah's fault that there was no rain? (No)
4. Could Baal make it rain? (No)
5. Did God make it rain? (Yes)
6. Can God do anything? (Yes)

Activities
1. Close your eyes and think about what rain sounds like.
2. Draw some clouds and rain.
3. Name some things that need rain to help them grow. (Ideas: trees, flowers, grass)

Prayer
Dear God, you are the same God who sent rain when Elijah prayed. You can do anything. Amen.

FIXING UP THE TEMPLE
2 Chronicles 36:1-23

May the Lord your God be with you. *2 Chronicles 36:23*

Josiah was eight years old when he was crowned king. Josiah loved God. For 31 years he did good things for his people. But the kings who lived after Josiah didn't care about God.

_____ , God sent many messengers to tell his people to stop doing wrong. But the kings made fun of God's messengers. They didn't listen.

So God let the king of another country called Babylon come over to attack the Jewish people. The king of Babylon burned down their beautiful temple, and the Babylonians made slaves of the Jewish people.

Then, after seventy long years, something good happened. A king from another country came over to Babylon. He said, "All you Jewish people are free now. You don't have to be slaves anymore. Go back to your city of Jerusalem and fix up God's temple. May God be with you." The Jewish people went back to Jerusalem and started once again to care about God and his temple. That was a wise decision.

Questions
1. Did the kings after Josiah care about God? (No)
2. What happened to the temple? (It was burned down.)
3. How long were the Jews slaves in Babylon? (Seventy years)
4. Did the Jewish people finally get to go free? (Yes)

Activity
Learn the last half of the verse together: "God be with you."

Prayer
Dear God, I want to be like Josiah. He loved you. Amen.

FINISHING THE JOB
Nehemiah 1 — 12

Celebrate with songs of thanksgiving. Nehemiah 12:27

Broken walls all around the city of Jerusalem made it hard for the people to stay safe. Nehemiah heard the sad news about his city and cried. But Nehemiah was a smart man. He decided to pray about his sadness. He wanted to fix the broken walls. Since Nehemiah had an important job in another city, he had to ask if he could leave and go to Jerusalem. Again, Nehemiah prayed. And he could go to Jerusalem.

Some people in Jerusalem made fun of Nehemiah and his workers. They tried to stop them from fixing the walls. But Nehemiah kept working. "All you workers," said Nehemiah, "don't be afraid! Remember God. He is great and he will help us."

Nehemiah was a good leader. God helped him. Finally, the walls of Jerusalem were finished. The people said, "We've worked hard to fix the wall. Now we give it to God as a gift." Then they sang thank-you songs to God. _____ , we can sing thank-you songs, too.

Questions
1. Who led the people to fix the wall? (Nehemiah)
2. Did Nehemiah pray for God's help? (Yes)

Activities
1. Pretend to build a wall with invisible blocks and hammer (or play with your toy blocks).
2. Sing a thank-you song.

Prayer
Dear God, you helped Nehemiah and the people build the wall even when others tried to stop them. Please help me when I have a hard time finishing what I start. Amen.

BEAUTIFUL QUEEN
Esther 2 — 8

You may have been chosen queen for just such a time as this.
Esther 4:14

There once was an important king named Xerxes. He had lots of money. He lived in a huge house called a palace. Many people worked for him. He wanted a wife, so he asked his workers to bring young women to meet him. A beautiful Jewish girl named Esther was one of the young women he met. "That's the one for me," he said. King Xerxes put a crown on Esther's head and had a big party to celebrate his marriage to her. Everybody seemed very happy.

But then something happened. One of the king's workers was a jealous, mean man. He decided to kill all the Jewish people. (Queen Esther was a Jew, and so was her family.) The news made Esther sad. So she put on her best queen's clothes and went to see the king. "Please let my people live," she begged. The king saved the Jewish people because of Queen Esther.

_____ , God helped Esther become the queen at just the right time. God always does the right thing at the right time. We can trust him to help us with everything we do.

Questions
1. What did King Xerxes want? (A wife)
2. Who became his new queen? (Esther)
3. Who helped save the Jewish people? (Queen Esther)

Activities
1. Pretend to crown your child king or queen.
2. Play "dress-up" like a king and queen.

Prayer
Dear God, Esther became queen so she could help her people. It was at just the right time. You always do things at just the right time. Amen.

IN HAPPY AND SAD TIMES
Job

God has said, ". . . I will never forget you." *Hebrews 13:5*

Job was a very good man. He always told the truth, and he stayed away from doing wrong things. He prayed for his children — seven grown sons and three daughters.

Job was also very rich. He had seven thousand sheep and three thousand camels. He had one thousand oxen and five hundred donkeys. He lived in a big house with many servants.

Job also loved God. _____ , you might think that Job loved God because God had given him so many good things. But Job loved God just because he is God.

One day bad things began to happen to Job. In a short time, because of fighting and lightning and more fighting and a terrible storm, Job lost his house, his animals, and his children. And then he got very sick, with sores all over his body.

But Job never stopped loving God. In fact, Job said, "I will always trust you, God." No matter what happened, Job would always love God.

God had not forgotten Job, even when the bad things happened. God honored Job because Job trusted him in happy times and in sad times. And God have Job happy times again.

Questions
1. Who was a very good man and very rich? (Job)
2. What happened to Job? (Everything he had was gone, and he got sick.)
3. Did God forget Job? (No)

Activity
Fill in the blank with your name. "God will never forget _____."

Prayer
Dear God, sometimes bad, sad things happen to me and to the people I love. But I know that in the happy or sad times you will not forget me. Thank you. Amen.

CHILDREN SING TO GOD
Psalm 8:1-9

You have taught children and babies to sing praises to you.
Psalm 8:2

Ryan and Nicole sat on the soft grass. They watched white puffy clouds move across the bright blue sky. "Look, the sun's hiding behind that funny-looking cloud," said Ryan.

"It's shaped like a bunny. See his little cottontail and floppy ears," said Nicole. "And look over there. 1-2-3-4-5-6. Six birds. I counted six birds!"

Ryan sat quietly. Then he said, "God makes great things for us to see, doesn't he? Remember that song we learned yesterday? Let's sing it! "

So Ryan and Nicole sang a song to God. In the song they praised God for the clouds and blue sky, the birds and the sweet-smelling grass, and the cows and chickens in the farmyard across the fence. We don't have to wait until we're grown up to praise and sing about God.

_____ , all children everywhere can sing to God.

Questions
1. Who are the children who praised God? (Ryan and Nicole)
2. Do we have to be grown up to sing to God? (No)
3. Who can sing to God? (All children everywhere)

Activities
1. Play the cloud game. Find different shaped clouds that look like things God has made.
2. Sing a song of praise together. Sing one you learned at church or make one up.

Prayer
Dear God, we praise you. You are so good! You make all the pretty things for us to see. Your name is the most wonderful name in all the earth. Amen.

I'M AFRAID!

Psalm 56:3, 4, 8-13

When I am afraid, I will trust you. Psalm 56:3

"Dad, sometimes when I'm at school, I feel afraid," whispered Tommy.

"There are times when I feel afraid, too," said Tommy's dad. "When I started my new job, I was afraid because I didn't know the people and I didn't know what I was supposed to do. And once when I was a boy I went camping. During the night it started to rain. The wind blew. The thunder boomed. I was scared. It helped when I said a Bible verse over and over again: 'When I am afraid, I will trust you. When I am afraid, I will trust you.' It really made me feel better to remember I could trust God."

When we're afraid, _____ , it's OK to say it. When we say we're afraid instead of pretending that we aren't, then we can ask God to help us. And he promised that he would always help us when we ask.

Questions
1. What did Tommy tell his dad? (Sometimes I'm afraid at school .)
2. Was Tommy's dad ever afraid? (Yes, when he started a new job.)
3. What verse did Tommy's dad say to himself when he was afraid as a child? ("When I am afraid, I will trust you.")

Activities
1. Make a sound like the wind. Make a sound like the thunder.
2. Write the verse "When I am afraid, I will trust you" in large letters on a sheet of paper. Cut into large puzzle pieces and then put the verse back together.

Prayer
Dear God, sometimes I am afraid. Please help me to remember to pray to you when I feel afraid. I know you will help me. Amen.

AS HIGH AS THE SKY
Psalm 103:11, 17

As high as the sky is above the earth, so great is his love
for those who respect him.
Psalm 103:11

"Does God love me?" asked Jimmy.

"Yes, God loves you very much," answered Jimmy's mom.

"But I mean does he really love me?" Jimmy asked again.

"I'm not fibbing," said his mom. "God really, really loves you
and me and Daddy and Grandma and baby sister Jenny."

"How much does God love us?" asked Jimmy.

"Well, Jimmy, let's walk outside," said Mom. "Look up. Can
you reach to the blue sky?"

"That's silly," said Jimmy. "You know I can't. It's higher than I
can even think about."

"That's how much God loves you," said Mom. "He loves you
and me more than we can ever know. "

Jimmy smiled and hugged his mother. "That makes me feel
happy," he said.

God loves Jimmy and God loves you, _____. As high as
the sky is above our housetop is how much God loves us.

Questions
1. What did Jimmy ask his mother? ("Does God love me? How
   much?")
2. What did Jimmy's mom take him outside to see? (The blue sky)
2. Does God love us? (Yes)

Activities
1. Look up at the sky. Try to imagine how high it is.
2. Name people you know. God loves us all.

Prayer
Dear God, you love me all the time, more than I can understand.
That makes me smile. Amen.

Note to parents/teachers
Children need to be reassured of our love. For the next few nights,
perhaps you could whisper these words to your child before he
goes to sleep: "God loves you and so do I."

NEVER TOO TIRED!
Psalm 121

He who guards you never sleeps. Psalm 121:3

"Dad," shouted Davey. "Help me wrap Mom's present please." Davey was proud of the picture he had colored for his mother's birthday tomorrow.

"I'd like to, Davey, but I'm too tired right now," said Dad. "Let me rest for a minute."

"Oh, all right," said Davey. Then he saw his big sister's car turn the corner. He ran to meet her. "Will you help me wrap Mom's present?" he asked.

Kathy's arms were loaded with books. "Davey, I'm so tired. Can you wait?"

"I guess so," said Davey. He walked back into the house and saw Grandma sitting at the kitchen table. He moved close. "Grandma, can you help me wrap Mom's present?" he whispered.

"Not now, Davey, I have a headache. I just got too tired today."

Davey walked down the hall to his room. He looked at the picture he drew for Mom. He looked at the wrapping paper, tape, and scissors. "I need help," he mumbled. "Dad and Kathy are too tired. Grandma's head is too tired. I guess I won't get any help tonight."

Sometimes we get too tired to work or play. But guess what, _____? When we pray to God for help, he is *never* too tired. He always has energy and time to listen and help us.

Questions
1. Who needed help wrapping Mom's present? (Davey)
2. Does God ever get tired? (No)

Activity
Draw a picture. Give it to someone.

Prayer
Dear God, it's good news that you are never too tired to help me. I love you for that. Amen.

THE "OBEY" NECKLACE
Proverbs 6:20-23

Remember [your parents'] words forever . . . as if they were tied around your neck. Proverbs 6:21

Come here, _____ , so I can give you a big hug and kiss. I want you to know that I love you very much. Because I love you, I have to tell you to do things you don't want to do.

Sometimes I have to tell you to take a bath or to come in from outside or to take a rest. I can't let you play in the street because a car might come and hurt you. I need to tell you to wear a coat when it's cold outside. I tell you to take a nap so you won't be too tired and grouchy at dinner. I do these things because I care about you.

God knows I care about you. The Bible says, "Listen to your mom and dad. Remember their words. Pretend to make a necklace out of the words they say. Pretend to wear it around your neck so you won't forget to obey."

Playing with your "pretend" necklace on will help you remember to obey. Obeying mom and dad will help keep you safe.

Questions
1. _____ , who loves you very much? (Mom, Dad, God, Grandma, Grandpa, brother, sister)
2. Whom does God tell you to obey? (Mom and Dad)

Activity
Help your child make a necklace. String popped popcorn, uncooked macaroni, or round oat cereal on a piece of yarn or twine that is long enough to fit over your child's head when tied together.

Prayer
Dear God, thank you that my parents love me. Help me to please you and them by obeying. Amen.

I'LL GO!
Isaiah 6:8-10; 7:14; 9:6; 53:3-12

The Lord had said through the prophet, ". . . She will have a son."
Matthew 1:22, 23

Many years ago, God asked a man named Isaiah two important questions, "Whom can I send?" and "Who will go for us?"

"I'm here. I'll go! Send me!" answered Isaiah. God wanted a man who loved him to help send a special message to the people. Isaiah decided to say "yes." He became God's prophet. God wanted his people to come back and love and believe him again. But the people were stubborn and selfish. They didn't listen to Isaiah's words.

God gave Isaiah these important words to tell the people. "Someday a special baby boy will be born," said Isaiah. "There will be no one else like him. He'll love all people. He'll make people well. He will grow up and take the punishment for the bad things people have done."

_____ , the special baby boy that Isaiah talked about was Jesus. These words were written down in the Bible long before Jesus was born.

Questions
1. Who said, "I will go! Send me!"? (Isaiah)
2. Who was the baby boy that Isaiah talked about many years before he was born? (Jesus)

Activity
Look at your Bible's table of contents. Find Isaiah, turn to the page, and show it to your child.

Prayer
Dear God, thank you for the special words about Jesus that you gave to Isaiah. Thank you that he wrote them down. It helps us to believe. Amen.

THE BURNED-UP LETTER
Jeremiah 36

My people, listen to my teaching. Listen to what I say. Psalm 78:1

_____ , have you ever written a letter? Long ago a man of God, named Jeremiah, wrote an important letter to the king. It was God's idea to send the letter. God told Jeremiah just what to write. The letter said, "Dear king and people in the kingdom, God says that armies from the north are coming to hurt you. If you stop doing wicked things and decide to love God again, then God will forgive you for the evil things you've done."

Jeremiah wrote other things in this letter, too. It made the people stop and think. Some of the people were afraid and sorry when they heard it. But the king was not sad. He didn't care about God. Do you know what he did? He took the letter and held it over a fire. Zap! The letter burned up! It was the king's way of saying, "I don't care what God says!"

It is a sad thing when people don't listen to God's words. Yet it is a happy thing when people decide to listen and obey God's words. When we read Bible stories, we learn about God and his wise words.

Questions
1. Who sent a letter to the king? (Jeremiah)
2. What did the king do with the letter? (Burned it up)

Activities
1. Plan to write a letter to someone you love.
2. Write the planned letter. Put a stamp on it. Put it in the mail.

Prayer
Dear God, your Bible is your letter to me. Help me always to listen and obey your words. Amen.

THE SECRET DREAM
Daniel 2:1-23

Daniel asked his friends to pray. *Daniel 2:18*

_____ , have you ever dreamed while you were sleeping? Sometimes we dream, don't we? In Bible times, dreams often meant something special.

King Nebuchadnezzar dreamed a strange dream. He wanted help in understanding what it meant. But the king wouldn't tell anyone about his dream. He wanted his "smart" helpers to guess what happened in his dream. He wanted them to tell him what it meant. But no one could do that. This made King Nebuchadnezzar angry!

Daniel heard about the king's anger and told his three friends. Daniel asked his friends to pray. "Ask God to help us understand the secret dream," he said.

That night while Daniel slept, God told him about the secret dream. When Daniel woke up, he said, "Thanks, God. You told me about the king's dream just like we asked you to do."

God listened to the young men's prayer. He answered their prayers. God listens to and answers our prayers, too.

Questions
1. Who had a strange dream? (King Nebuchadnezzar)
2. Could his helpers tell him what it meant? (No)
3. Who prayed to God for help? (Daniel and his three friends)

Activities
1. Draw a picture of Daniel and his three friends praying to God.
2. Draw a picture of your friends and you praying to God.

Prayer
Dear God, help me to remember to pray when I need help. Amen.

A SECRET NO LONGER
Daniel 2:24-49

Lord, you know everything. John 21:17

_____ , King Nebuchadnezzar was angry when no one could tell him what his dream meant. Then brave Daniel came before the angry king. "Can you tell me about my dream and what it means?" asked the king.

"Nobody could do that," said Daniel. "Only God in Heaven is wise enough to know secret things. I'm no smarter than the others. God's the one who told me the secret, but I'll share it will you." Daniel told King Nebuchadnezzar the dream and explained what it meant.

"Now I see that your God is the greatest," said the king. "He tells you secret things. I know what you say must be true." The king gave Daniel gifts and put him in charge of all the helpers.

Daniel became an important leader. Daniel asked the king if his three friends could have important jobs, too. The happy king said yes. Daniel had the courage to face the king and talk about God. God helped Daniel and he will help us, too.

Questions
1. Who went before the king? (Brave Daniel)
2. Who is the one who told Daniel about the dream? (God)
3. Who made Daniel an important leader? (King Nebuchadnezzar)

Activities
1. Whisper a message in your child's ear. (Ideas: I love you; God loves you; you have pretty eyes; your hair is shiny.)
2. Write the verse above on a piece of paper. Color it. Hang it up in your room.

Prayer
Dear God, you helped Daniel. You are the one who helps me, too. Thank you. Amen.

NO HIDING FROM GOD
Jonah 1:4 — 2:1, 10; 3:3

Nothing in all the world can be hidden from God.
Hebrews 4:13

_____ , do you see the boat in the picture? Jonah ran away and hid in a boat like this. God had asked Jonah to do something special, and Jonah didn't want to. Then a big storm came. The boat's sailors were afraid. The wind blew harder and harder, but Jonah slept. "Hey, man, get up!" said the captain. "Start praying. We need help! Quick!"

All the sailors got together to try to figure out why such a bad storm came. "Is it because of someone on this boat?" they asked.

"It's probably because of me," said Jonah. "I thought I could hide from God. Now I know I can't. Pick me up and throw me over the side. Then the storm will go away."

The sailors began to pray to God for the first time in their lives. When they threw Jonah into the water, the storm stopped. After all this happened, the men believed in God.

God sent a big fish to swallow Jonah while he swam in the water. Jonah stayed safe in the fish's stomach. There he prayed. After three nights the fish spit Jonah out. So Jonah dried off and went where God had asked him to go. Jonah had decided to do what God asked him to do.

God was with the sailors in the boat and Jonah in the water. He was with Jonah in the fish. And God is with us right now. There is no place we can go where he can't see us, help us, and love us. That's good news.

Questions
1. Who thought he could run away from God? (Jonah)
2. What did God send to swallow Jonah? (A big fish)
3. Can we hide from God? (No)

Activities
1. Pretend your bed or chair is a rocking boat.
2. Draw a picture of a boat. Put waves in the water.

Prayer
Dear God, everywhere I go, you can see me and help me. That makes me feel good. Amen.

RUNNING AND HIDING
Jonah 1, 2

The Lord looks down from heaven. He sees every person.
Psalm 33:13

"Davey," called Mother. "Come inside and take your bath. We're going to Aunt Bessie's for dinner." Davey acted like he couldn't hear. "Davey, come in *right now!*" called Mom again.

Davey had an idea. "I'll hide. Then Mom won't find me. I don't want to go to Aunt Bessie's anyway. She doesn't have a TV. And she squeezes me too hard when she hugs me." So Davey ran down the street and hid behind the bushes at the park.

Soon it started to get dark. "Mom's probably looking for me," said Davey. He began to think it wasn't a good idea to run and hide. Davey thought about the story of Jonah, how Jonah tried to run and hide from God, but found out no one can hide from God. Davey remembered that God can see everywhere. He began to cry. "I'm sorry I didn't come inside when Mom called me," he told God. "I know I can't hide from you." So Davey ran home as fast as he could. He saw his mother in the yard looking for him.

"Where were you, Davey?" she asked.

"I was hiding. But I remembered Jonah. I told God I was sorry and I ran home."

"I'm glad you're safe, Davey." She hugged him. "Please don't ever run away again."

Questions
1. Who tried to hide from his mom? (Davey)
2. Whom did Davey tell he was sorry? (God and his mom)

Activity
Think up an ending to the story. Did Davey go to Aunt Bessie's? Were they late? Was Davey punished for disobeying Mom?

Prayer
Dear God, thank you for seeing, loving, and forgiving me. Amen.

RYAN, THE PRAYING BOY
Daniel 2:18, 20; Daniel 6:10

Never stop praying. *1 Thessalonians 5:17*

Daniel went to his upstairs room and prayed to God three times each day. He knew it was important to talk to God about everything. Daniel was a praying man who lived many years ago.

Ryan is a praying boy who lives today. Like Daniel, he thinks it's important to talk to God. One night he said, "Mom, I'm going to pray for Aunt Joanie tonight. I'll pray that she'll write the children's Bible stories fast. Then all the boys and girls will hear about God and his Son, Jesus." The next day, Ryan remembered his prayer. He prayed when he woke up. He prayed at noon time. He prayed at night time.

Aunt Joanie smiled when she learned about Ryan's prayers. Aunt Joanie and Ryan didn't get to visit often because they lived far away from one another. Yet they both knew that God listened to them every time they prayed.

_____ , God listens to us. He listened to Daniel a long time ago. He listens to us today. God is pleased when we pray.

Questions
1. Who was the praying man? (Daniel)
2. Who was the praying boy? (Ryan)
3. Whom did Ryan pray for? (Aunt Joanie)
4. Did God hear Ryan's prayers? (Yes)

Activity
Look at a map. Find where you live. Find where a faraway friend or relative lives.

Prayer
Dear God, I like to pray to you. Help me never to stop praying and believing you. Amen.

MICAH, THE TRUTH TELLER
Micah

But from you [Bethlehem] will come one who will rule Israel.
Micah 5:2

_____ , do you remember the man who was swallowed by the big fish? He was a prophet of God named Jonah. A prophet tells people about God's plans. God had another prophet named Micah. The words of Micah are written down in the Bible book called Micah.

"I'm not fooling around. I'm telling the truth here," Micah said. "God loves you. But you've stopped praying. You do such bad things. It makes me sad. And it makes God sad, too."

"Don't talk to us like that," said the people. "We won't listen to anything except nice words. Even if you have to lie, tell us nice words."

Still Micah told the truth. Sometimes it feels sad to hear the truth — especially when the truth is that we disobeyed. "Because you follow the evil king's way," said Micah, "God is going to let your city be torn down by other countries. Someday though you will come back to God."

Micah wrote about God, his fairness, and his promises. He wrote about God's plan to send Jesus to be our Savior.

Questions
1. Who were the two prophets? (Jonah and Micah)
2. What is a prophet? (A person who tells others about God's plans)
3. Who stopped praying to the God who loved them? (The people)

Activities
Count the letters that are the same in the names Jonah and Micah.

Prayer
Dear God, Micah told the truth, even when the people didn't like it. Help me to tell the truth, even when it is hard to do. Amen.

DECIDING TO CARE
Nahum

So now, those who are in Christ Jesus are not judged guilty.
Romans 8:1

When Jonah preached in Nineveh, the people prayed. God heard their prayers and stopped the city from being torn down. Many years later, a prophet named Nahum went to Nineveh, too. Nahum said, "God is good. He doesn't get mad quickly. He cares about people. Still, when people do bad things over and over again, God has to stop it. This is because God is fair."

The people of Nineveh hadn't keep their promise. They had stopped praying. They had stopped caring. God loved them, but they didn't care. They hurt many people, but they didn't care. So God told the prophet Nahum that Nineveh would be torn down this time for certain.

It is sad when people decide not to care about God. The happy choice is to love and care about God and his ideas. _____, God promises to help us when we make this smart decision.

Questions
1. Who said "God is good, but he cannot let people do bad things over and over"? (Nahum)
2. Who had stopped praying and caring? (The people of Nineveh)
3. What is the wise choice? (To love and care about God and his ideas)

Activities
1. Name some of the laws of your city.
2. Name some of God's laws.

Prayer
Dear God, we can't break the rules of our city. And we can't break your rules over and over again, either. You are very fair. And you are loving. Amen.

GOD SEES EVERYWHERE
Acts 10:1-8

The Lord . . . sees every person. . . . He watches everyone.
Psalm 33:13, 14

_____ , you live in the city of _____ . Another child about your age lives in the city of _____ (name a city nearby.) You don't know each other, but God sees and knows you both.

Peter lived in Joppa. A man named Cornelius lived in Caesarea. They didn't know each other. But God saw Peter and cared about him. And God saw Cornelius and cared about him. Cornelius loved and prayed to God. He showed he loved God by sharing with poor people. One day an angel came to Cornelius. "What do you want?" asked surprised Cornelius.

"God hears you every time you pray," said the angel. "He's happy you give to the poor. God wants to tell you some important things. In Joppa, there is another man who prays to God. His name is Simon Peter. Send some men to get him. He'll come and tell you what God wants you to know." When the angel left, Cornelius's men went to find Peter.

God could see Peter and Cornelius. God sees every person. He never closes his eyes. He doesn't have to, because he never gets tired. He can see and help lots of people at the same time. God is *omnipresent*.

Questions
1. Where did Peter live? (Joppa)
2. Where did Cornelius live? (Caesarea)
3. Where do you live?

Activities
1. Pretend to be Cornelius when the angel came.
2. Look at a map together and point to several cities.

Prayer
Dear God, I know you can see my friend from another city and me at the same time. No one is like you. Amen.

PETER'S TRIP
Acts 10:9-23

I have promised to obey your words.
Psalm 119:57

_____ , a long time ago, houses had steps that went to the roof. One day, Peter climbed the steps to his roof. He wanted a quiet place to pray. While Peter was on the roof, he had a vision, something like a dream. As he was thinking about the vision, Cornelius's men came.

Just then God's Holy Spirit said to Peter, "Three men are downstairs looking for you. Go with them. I sent them to get you."

Peter asked the men to stay all night. And the next morning, Peter and the men left to go see Cornelius. Peter did not know why he was going; Cornelius did not know why Peter was coming. Both men did what God said anyway. They believed that God was doing something good.

Questions
1. Where did Peter go to pray? (To the roof)
2. Who came to Peter's house? (The three men Cornelius sent)
3. Did Peter go with the three men? (Yes)

Activity
Take your fingers and walk them up your child's arm and shoulder to the top of his head, like Peter walked up to his roof.

Prayer
Dear God, Peter and Cornelius didn't know exactly why you wanted them to meet. But they obeyed anyway. Help me to obey you, too. Amen.

WHO'S KNEELING?
Acts 10:24-33

It does not belong to us, Lord. The praise belongs to you.
Psalm 115:1

Knock! Knock! Cornelius ran to open the door. There stood Peter. Right away, Cornelius knelt in front of Peter. He tried to worship Peter. But Peter said, "Oh, Cornelius, please get up. I'm not God. I'm a man just like you. Don't worship me."

"Peter, please come in. Meet my family and friends," said Cornelius.

Peter looked at all the people. "I've never been in the house of a person who is not a Jew. I always thought it was wrong. But God just told me that all people are loved and accepted by him. I came to visit because God said it was OK. Now, tell me, why did you want me to come?"

"Four days ago, when I was praying to God, an angel came to me," answered Cornelius. "He told me to ask you to come visit. Now you're here and I'm glad. Tell us about God."

Peter shared with Cornelius, his family, and friends. Peter was God's helper. But Peter was not God. _____ , we do not kneel down to worship another person. God is the one we worship.

Questions
1. Who visited Cornelius? (Peter)
2. Who knelt down to worship Peter? (Cornelius)
3. What did Peter say? ("Please get up. Don't worship me. I'm not God.")

Activity
Knock on a nearby table. Pretend to open the door to a visitor. Introduce yourself. Do a short dialogue with your child.

Prayer
Dear God, I know it's good for me to worship and pray to you only. Amen.

GOD IS THE BEST
Acts 12:18-23

Lord my God, you are very great. You are clothed with glory and majesty. Psalm 104:1

_____ , can you guess what happened when Herod the king found out Peter wasn't in jail anymore? He was angry. He looked for Peter, but couldn't find him. Peter had gone away.

One day after this, Herod put on special fancy clothes and sat down on a big throne. He called all the people together to listen to him talk.

Herod talked as if he were the one who had done great and wonderful things. He did not praise God. He wanted people to think he was bigger and better than God.

"Herod is not just a man; he is a god!" shouted the people.

Herod could have decided to praise God, but he didn't. Herod made a bad decision.

It is good to praise God. He is the greatest of all leaders.

Questions
1. Did Herod love God? (No)
2. Did Peter love God? (Yes)
3. What did the people shout about Herod? ("Herod is not just a man; he is a god!")
4. Who is the best? (God)

Activities
1. Make an angry face (like the king). Make a kind face (like Peter).
2. Pretend you are a king. Dress in a robe and sit in a big chair. Talk to your people. But tell them to love and praise God.

Prayer
Dear God, no one is greater than you. You are the one who made all the world. You are the one who helps us. Thank you. Amen.

WILL GRANDMA COME?
Philippians 4:6

Do not worry about anything. But pray and ask God for everything you need. Philippians 4:6

Jeffy pulled the covers over his head. "Mommy, what if Grandma doesn't come?" he whispered. "What if she gets sick? What if she has a wreck?"

"My, Jeffy, that's a lot to think about," said Mom. "She promised to stay with you while Daddy and I are gone. She'll come. You'll see." Mommy kissed Jeffy good-night.

Jeffy stared at the ceiling. Who would stay with him if Grandma didn't come? "Dear God," prayed Jeffy. "I need Grandma to stay with me. Help her to come. Amen." Then Jeffy saw his little Bible on the night table. "Grandma will come," he said. "I know she will." Soon Jeffy forgot his worries and fell asleep.

_____ , God helped Jeffy. God will help us, too. He hears us when we pray.

Questions
1. Who prayed to God for help? (Jeffy)
2. Did God help Jeffy to stop worrying and go to sleep? (Yes)
3. Do you think Grandma came the next day?

Activities
1. Talk about what you and your child might do tomorrow.
2. Draw a picture for your child's grandma or grandpa.

Prayer
Dear God, sometimes when I'm afraid I start to worry. Help me to remember to pray and ask you to help me to stay calm. Amen.

LETTER TO A SON
2 Timothy 1:3-8; 4:13, 17, 18

He gave us a spirit of power and love and self-control.
2 Timothy 1:7

_____ , Paul had a young friend named Timothy. They loved each other. When they couldn't be together, they wrote letters. From jail Paul wrote Timothy this letter:

Dear Timothy, you are like a special son to me. I pray for you all the time. I know you love God like I do. I'm glad your mom and grandma taught you about God while you were growing up.

I just wanted to remind you what our God is like. God doesn't want us to be afraid. He isn't the one who makes us scared to tell the truth or meet new friends or learn new things. Sometimes other people may try to make us feel afraid of them. But God is never like that.

God gives us courage to do and say the right thing. He gives us love for others and ourselves. God helps us when we need to learn to wait or do hard jobs. We don't have to be afraid to tell other people that we love God, because he will give us strength to talk about it at the right time.

I've missed my friends while I've been here in prison, but I know God has been with me always. One day soon I'm going to go live with him in Heaven. Come visit me here, if you can. **Love, Paul.**

Questions
1. Who wrote a letter to young Timothy? (Paul)
2. Does God want us to be afraid to tell the truth, meet new friends, or learn new things? (No)

Activity
Write a letter or draw a picture and send it to a friend.

Prayer
Dear God, you're wonderful. I know you give me courage, love, and patience. Thanks. Amen.

HAVE YOU EVER SEEN GOD?
Colossians 1:15-20

No one has seen God, but Jesus is exactly like him. *Colossians 1:15*

"Dad, have you ever seen God?" asked Scotty.

"No," said Dad. "I never have."

"Has Pastor Barnes ever seen God?" Scotty asked.

"No, Scotty, Pastor Barnes hasn't seen God, either."

"Has anybody ever seen him, then?"

"No, nobody here on earth has seen God," answered Dad.

"Well, how are we supposed to know what he's like, then?" asked Scotty.

"That's one reason why Jesus came here," said Dad. "Everything Jesus said or did helps us know what God is like."

"You mean when you tell me stories about Jesus you are really telling about God?"

"You could say that, Scotty," said Dad. "Jesus did many wonderful things when he lived here on earth. He was loving, fair, and wise. Just like God. And when he died and came back to life, he helped us become friends with God."

Questions
1. Has anyone ever seen God? (No)
2. Who helps us to know what God is like? (Jesus)

Activity
Make a verbal list of the good things about Jesus. (Ideas: He loved children; he cared about sick people; he had good friends; he was never in a hurry; he prayed.)

Prayer
Dear God, I know that I can't see you, but I know that you are there. I want to learn more about Jesus, so I can know what you are like. Help me. Amen. Love, ~~VANICA~~ .